But,

Couldn't I Do That?

Answering Your Questions About Self-Publishing

But,

Couldn't I Do That?

Answering Your Questions About Self-Publishing

Erin O'Neil & Scott Ryan

Fishtail Publishing

Cover photo by Erin O'Neil
Front & back covers designed by Erin O'Neil and Scott Ryan
Edited by Courtenay Stallings
Book designed by Scott Ryan
Graphics by Erin O'Neil

Published in the USA by Fishtail Publishing, LLC
Reynoldsburg, Ohio

Contact Information
Email: fishtailpublishing@gmail.com
Website: fishtailpublishing.org

ISBN: 9781733338080

"I'll be as brief as possible, because your time is valuable and so is mine, and we both understand that the hours we spend talking about writing is time we don't spend actually doing it."
 – Stephen King, *On Writing*

"Where's passion in the art, where's craft?"
 – Stephen Sondheim, "Liaisons" from *A Little Night Music*

CONTENTS

Introduction...1

Chapter 1: How Did Erin Do That?...............................5

Chapter 2: How Did Scott Do That?............................10

Chapter 3: How Do I Develop a Story?........................17

Chapter 4: Why Self-Publishing?................................29

Chapter 5: How Do I Design a Cover?.........................46

Chapter 6: How Do I Promote My Book?....................56

Chapter 7: Which Software Should I Use?...................68

Chapter 8: What Makes a Good Book Design?............78

Chapter 9: What About ISBNs, Barcodes, and Copyrights?...................87

Chapter 10: What Else Do I Need?..............................99

Chapter 11: Can You Tell Me One More Time?.........111

Chapter 12: But, Can I Really Do This?.....................115

Appendix A: What Do Other Authors Have To Say?...........120

About The Authors...130

Introduction

If you are here, you probably have an idea for a book but are filled with questions. An idea is a start, but there are many tasks to complete to get that idea from your mind to a reader's book shelf, Kindle, phone, or implanted memory chip. (Who knows how people will be consuming books by the time you are reading this.) If you are lucky enough to have your idea in manuscript form, then you are in better shape than someone who is just thinking about getting that idea out of their head. Maybe you are super lucky and you already have a manuscript and publisher interested in your work. No matter where you are in the process, we are ready to help. From idea to finished product is a long, hard road. There will be many off ramps that will make you want to turn off the highway and get back to safety. Take none of them.

The goal of this book is to walk through the process of publishing and share the path that took us from unpublished *and unknown*, to published and unknown. (Hey, it was a start.) Between us we have covered the gamut of publishing. Scott Ryan has published with a traditional publisher and self-published. Erin O'Neil has self-published and now councils other authors on the art of self-publishing. Both of us have edited, designed, and distributed our own books as well as books for multiple other authors. We've seen it all, and we're still here. In this book, we share with you how we did it and what we learned. It's a gold mine of experiences.

We both agree that it was our drive and love of creating art that helped push us through to the end, however, the key element in both of our stories is one thing in particular—kindness. Self-publishing can be a frustrating, time-consuming, and often grueling process. It can be easy to have an end goal so clear that all the other details become muddled or stressful. So, before taking on the challenge of self-publishing, consider the ways in which you might approach adversity and collaborate with others to make your goal a success. Kindness is the foundation for achieving productive and intentional collaboration with anyone who helps make your book a success.

Later in the book, once you get to know us and love us, we will tell you the story of how we met as strangers in line for free coffee, and the friendship we forged at a Panera (or Bread Co., depending on where you're from). But this openness and kindness is how we each have succeeded in business. Every day and every step forward there is always a large corporation that tries to do its best to crush any little author or publisher. That is *their* business. *Your* business is to be firm with the big guys and kind with the little ones.

You are going to need designers, editors, photographers, web designers, customer service representatives, printers, salesmen, postal employees and co-authors. Most likely, you will not have money to pay for all of these services, so creating a nexus of kindness and getting the help and assistance of strangers is your best way to succeed. A quick Scott story…

•••••

Scott: Part of being a self-publisher, who does 100% of my direct sales on the internet, means I spend a lot of time at the post office shipping my products. Depending on your level of success for pre-orders, you may end up being there longer than you think. The longest time I spent shipping one of my company's books (*Laura's Ghost: Women Speak about Twin Peaks*) was five and a half hours. That is 330 minutes I spent at the post office. I am not exaggerating. I actually brought a chair with me. I couldn't have gotten through those hours at the post office if it wasn't for my relationship with the post office staff.

If you are managing your own shipping, you are going to spend some time learning when to ship via media mail or large envelope, when you need a customs form, and when it is best to use two-day priority mail to get the bulk rate. Here is an early tip: If your envelope has bubbles on it, it will always be more expensive than one that doesn't because of the machines it has to travel through to be postmarked. It's the difference between the postage being a large envelope or a package. These are things I have learned by going to the post office four times a week for the past five years. This learning curve can be difficult and stressful, but if you form a good relationship with those who can teach you, you'll have a much better time of it.

I have made it a point to make friends with each and every person who has waited on me at the post office. I ask them about their day. I come in prepared with a fun story to tell. And I am always ready when I approach the counter (I have each custom form filled out, all labels and addresses on the package). While I am friendly and friends with everyone who works at the post office, no one is better to me than my postal BFF, Shameeka. When it's a new book release day, and I have a lot of packages, I bring her coffee and a Starbucks cake pop. I have even ordered her favorite chips from her hometown and brought them in. I gave her copies of my books. I also bring treats for the other workers because they are going to have to be more efficient with the other customers while I am monopolizing Shameeka's time. I made the post office experience fun. I have walked into the place when it is dead quiet and left with everyone in line arguing about whether or not you can call Bob Evans fast food. (You can't.)

Everywhere you go, make the people behind the counter smile. Not just because you need their help, but because they're human, and they're trying to get a job done just as you are. Plus, if you are successful and have to ship out three hundred books in one day, you are going to want that employee to help you and be sure that your time is well spent. If a package is lost, Shameeka always helps me find it. I have seen other customers come in and yell, then be honestly surprised the postal worker doesn't want to help.

This type of kindness and humanity is what will set you apart from others. It makes people want to work with you. If you are having someone design your cover for you, be kind when they return their first draft with something you absolutely hate. Don't tell them they suck. Tell them you get what they were trying to conceptualize, but take ownership for not communicating clearly what your vision was. Also be open to the fact that you might not understand everything about creating a cover and listen before you react. You aren't going to get the best out of someone whom you beat down. Most people who you interact with are artists and creatives. They need a little boost and some encouragement. Even when you are dealing with a customer service rep on the phone, be kind. Everything I've ever gotten out of life, I got because I was kind to someone.

•••••

In this book, we are going to share with you what we have learned. We will give you the best of what we did. We will give you the mistakes we learned from, and the successes and failures we've experienced. Take our experiences and advice and make something from it. We are still learning and growing, and neither of us has a servant following us everywhere and getting us Mai Tais when we are thirsty. But we are going to keep working until that happens. (I just asked Scott to get me one, and he said no, so I guess I am not there yet.)

Each chapter is designed around a critical question because we were overwhelmed with questions when we first began this journey. The majority of our advice is for someone who is going to self-publish because if you have a big time publisher, they are probably going to handle most of the nitty-gritty work. Chapters 1-2 explain how we got here, so you know our background. In Chapters 3-10, we walk you through the process. We summarize our guidelines in Chapter 11 with a short and sweet outline for quick and easy reference. Then we send you on your way in Chapter 12. We finish up with an appendix that includes the experiences and advice of other authors who have diverse experiences, including self-publishing and publishing with a corporation. We provide this so you have more than one path to choose from. There is not just one way to the library finish line. If you read this text in full, you will have the tools and insight to develop your own self-publishing strategy and see your idea through to the end.

Now that we have all of our kindness antennas up and ready to go. Turn the page and start learning how to publish your book.

CHAPTER ONE

How Did Erin Do That?

I will never forget sitting across from one of my idols as she held up her copy of my first book. While she wasn't in the publishing or writing industry, she was a strong, capable, and fearless female leader and business owner, so her opinion mattered to me. She gushed over the cover design and casually flipped through the pages before looking me dead in the eyes and saying, "I hope you look back on this book years from now and feel embarrassed." My stomach squeezed its way up into my throat, and I'm pretty sure my kneecaps melted down into my shoes. *Excuse me?* I sat in a stunned silence as my role model nonchalantly informed me my work will one day suck—if it doesn't already.

Had I known then what I know now, I might have shaken her hand and thanked her graciously. At the time, however, this comment left me questioning every second I had spent over the last year writing, editing, restructuring, and designing this book on my own. Maybe if I had spent my energy publishing traditionally, she wouldn't be giving me the same advice. I was proud to have pulled off self-publishing a semi-professional publication. Going back to that moment a year and a half later, I realize what she had given me was actually a gift; humility.

What she was really saying was that if I don't look back on that first book now and laugh, I've done something horribly wrong. It would mean one of two things; either I have failed to learn and progress in the industry despite years having passed by, or my ego is unfathomably oversized. Neither would be ideal. Although I'm not quite to the point of laughter or embarrassment, I can already admit I would have done things differently. *Gui Ren: Extraordinary Stories of Ordinary People* was published over a year ago, and I am no longer the writer nor the publisher I was then.

I published my first book when I was 7 years old. It was one of those do-it-yourself children's publication kits that came with illustration paper and cheap washable markers. I spent days at our dining room table perfecting the poems, doodling images that made more sense in my head than on paper, and telling my entire family I was going to be the youngest published author the world had ever seen. My family gushed over it, encouraging my artistic expression and saluting my determination to make history. (Dorothy Straight, of course, had me beat forty years prior to my accomplishment, publishing her book at four years old. But I was a 7-year-old living in my own world.) The point is, if I still thought that my first book was a golden work of art, I probably wouldn't be in the publishing business today. No one would be interested in a 7-year-old's doodles on their book cover. Instead, I've continued to learn from mistakes, grow as a writer, and develop my voice. I laugh at that book of poetry now, and I deeply appreciate the ability to do so.

When I graduated from college, I temporarily relocated overseas to Shanghai, China to pursue a short-term work opportunity that would connect me to business leaders and entrepreneurs from all over the world. Despite having worked with the client before as an intern, my post-graduate experience was hardly the same. I found myself in a toxic work environment with little hope for improvement. When I made the difficult decision to end our contract early and instead spend my last few months abroad traveling around Southeast Asia, I inevitably created a new path for myself and my creative capacities.

Throughout my adventures I published blog posts as a means of documentation for myself and casual entertainment for others. I wrote short pieces about people, places, and experiences that were charming, heart-warming, and often comical in nature. I had no intention of turning my blog into anything noteworthy. The 200 followers of my Facebook page were compliment enough. Yet, somehow, when the right people got hold of my musings, they encouraged me to take things one step further. One day someone commented on one of my blog posts, "If you wrote a book, I would read it." Although I had the passing thought of printing my blog posts in a small paperback book just to stick on my bookshelf next to my other travel journals, I never saw myself turning it into a publication complete with an ISBN or copyright page. I didn't have a degree in English, nor had I ever published anything beyond that 7-year-old's doodle-filled book of poetry.

It was on an overnight train to Singapore when I opened my laptop and started writing what would shortly become the introduction to *Gui Ren*. As I watched the beginnings of a greater work spill onto the screen of my MacBook Pro, I made the decision. I've tried to write several books in my short lifetime, even tried my hand at a memoir at 15 years old. Each of those projects were quickly abandoned as I realized I didn't have a complete story to tell. Sitting on that train at 2 o'clock in the morning, with my hiking pack nestled against me, I knew this time was different. Most of the stories were already documented in some way—some in vlog format, others in blog posts, and a few mere Instagram posts—and there was much more to the story I could add in the development. As I began developing my content, I discovered the urge to elaborate and paint a more vivid picture. I wanted to really bring the reader into my world, illustrate the experiences, and immerse them in the thoughts and emotions of a solo female traveler. However, having never written a book before, my conceptualization of what that might look like was different from someone with decades of experience in the world of writing and publishing.

My first word of advice is also my first expression of gratitude: Find yourself a Susanne Jaffe. Susanne was my wonderful editor who spent hours with me revising and clarifying my work. She is also the very reason my soon-to-be-husband wrote the epilogue, which ultimately became one of my favorite parts of the story as a whole. She embraced my artistic creation and managed to wrap a beautiful bow around it. Whether you follow any of the other advice in this book, at a minimum, hire a good editor. They will not only make your story more comprehendible to the reader, but editors may find inspirations you hadn't yet noticed in your own work.

Reflecting on my process for publishing, it's no wonder I can already laugh at the formatting of *Gui Ren*; I did it entirely in Microsoft Word. There's nothing wrong with this method, of course. It's not impossible to produce a professional book with the simplest of software. However, it didn't give me a great idea of what the final product would truly look like. I had to rely on Amazon's author proof copies for that. I selected Amazon as my platform for several reasons, but primarily because when people became slightly confused by my preorder process, they messaged me saying they couldn't locate the title on Amazon. So, I chose my distributor based on where everyone was already looking for copies. It was that simple. There was also the issue of returns processing, but you'll read about that later on.

Gui Ren was the result of long hours of writing at the Starbucks near my childhood home, even longer hours making revisions and restructuring the chapters, and plenty of hype from family members and friends. It was the culmination of afternoons spent revisiting the quiet streets of Luang Prabang or bustling marketplaces of Bangkok, and recreating the moments by stringing just the right words together on a blank canvas. It was an artistic recreation of my time abroad that wove together reality with reflection. It was, quite frankly, a hodgepodge of "making shit work when it didn't want to" by fudging the formatting process and faking my way through with confidence. If I didn't know how to hide page numbers on certain sections, I covered them with a white square and exported it as a flattened PDF. Above all, I figured out how to make it work.

Within a few weeks of launch, I sold over 200 copies and broke even on my investment in Amazon's pay-per-print service. I signed up for author events and book signings, and kept copies in my car in case of emergencies. The latter came in handy on several surprising occasions (at the gym, at work, or walking out of the grocery store). It wasn't quite bestseller status, but I held onto that pride of short-term success. It is still, to this day, one of the coolest things I've ever done.

Most of my time outside of writing was spent researching, asking questions, talking to other authors, asking other business owners about their practices, and watching YouTube videos about book design and publishing platforms. I frequently found myself heading down a path only to turn around, go back, and pick a new route. I went into self-publishing with an open mind and zero expectations. Because of this, I gained valuable insight and learned to adapt in the face of challenges. I am still learning, and I am constantly navigating changing technologies and an evolving industry. I felt empowered by the process of self-publishing and appreciated the freedom to represent myself and my experiences with full agency and authenticity. After publishing my first book, I began using my skills to provide other authors with the tools they need to self-publish. My mission since is amplifying voices, encouraging the exploration of storytelling, and empowering artists to put their work into the world with intent and pride.

Self-publishing is not for everyone. It takes self-discipline, motivation, and drive. Self-publishing requires you to set aside what you think you know about the industry and start absorbing the experiences of others. It will challenge you to step outside your realm of knowledge and force you to think critically about the process from idea to printing. Decisions will be meticulous and plentiful. To me, this was invigorating and thrilling, but I realize it's not for everyone. That is why we, as authors and creators, must lean on each other for guidance and reassurance. That is why this book is in your hands or staring at you from a screen. I'm here for you. Scott is here for you. Together, between the two of us, we will illuminate the path to your first self-published work. And when the time comes when you look back on your first idea—your first publication—and laugh, we'll be there, too. And we will applaud you for it.

Chapter Takeaways

1. Don't publish a book because you want to publish a book. Publish a book because you have a story to tell.

2. Keep an open mind and open heart to the many words of advice, guidance, and insight from other authors and publishers. They are your allies.

3. Make sure you are up for the challenge. If you are not, surround yourself with people who can encourage your endeavor and provide support where you need it.

CHAPTER TWO

How Did Scott Do That?

I wish I could say I was an overnight success, but unfortunately it took forty-two years until I was published, and I have never had a financial bonanza. So I am neither overnight, nor a success, but my books have brought happiness to strangers, and they are in libraries and bookstores around the world. As a child, I wanted more than anything to be a writer, and that dream came true. Plus, what would I do with all that money, anyway? Eat? Who needs it. If I wanted to make money, I would have continued answering phones in a call center for a corporation. I am a writer and a creator. I have no choice in it. If you do, I suggest you do something else. I would if I could. I tried, and I can't.

I wrote my first book when I was ten years old. I wrote *Life in Timberline* right after my first girlfriend broke up with me. We had gone together for eight days, so it was a pretty big deal. I wrote my next one at sixteen when my first "real" girlfriend broke up with me. (I'm starting to sense a pattern.) After college, I wrote about my four years working at Arby's. Add it up and that meant that I wrote three novels by the time I was twenty. I wouldn't write another book for over twenty years. I started writing movies and making them with my friends. I did that for the next couple of decades. In the meantime, I got jobs, had kids, had wives, and lived life. It wasn't until I passed forty that I went back to writing books. In 2012, the name "Scott Ryan" was not listed on Amazon. It was not listed in any library, and no one ever paid any money to buy anything that

I had written. Writing this in 2021, I have been published in nineteen magazines, three essay books, and five full books. My work has shipped all around the globe and has been read in every country. (Remember, I still have not really made any money. I think if you totaled all of the profit, it would still be less money than I made during those four years at Arby's.) I have always been a writer, a storyteller, and an entertainer. It never mattered much to me what it brought back in the way of income. I was in it to make people laugh.

The thing I am most proud of is that through all the years, I never gave up. Oh, I got discouraged—I am *still* discouraged—but I never quit. I create a project and finish it based on the date I set, and then I start the next one. I never cared how it was received. I cared that I got the idea out. The first time I was ever published was in an essay book about the TV series *Twin Peaks*. I co-wrote the essay with my brother-in-law. That was in 2012. That same year, I submitted two articles to a magazine about Stephen Sondheim, and they both were published. So I went from nothing, to being in a book, *Fan Phenomena: Twin Peaks*, and a magazine, *The Sondheim Review*. I was finally a published author. I was paid nothing for the essay book and $100 for the articles. (Have I driven home the point, too much, that there really isn't money in this?)

In 2015, a writer whom I really respected reacted to and retweeted my tweet about a podcast episode I had done about the 1987 TV series *thirtysomething*. Richard Kramer was a writer on the series. I responded and asked him for an interview. He agreed. He guested on *The Red Room Podcast*, which I co-created with my brother-in-law, and asked me if I wanted to interview any of the actors from *thirtysomething*. I ended up interviewing the entire cast, the writers, and most of the directors. I even got to talk with Oscar-nominated director Ed Zwick (*Legends of the Fall, Glory*). This is how my first book began. I sent an email to Bear Manor Media because they published other books about classic TV shows. I wrote a very long pitch, listing all the people I interviewed, and my plans for the book. The owner responded back with one word: Sold. In 2017, *thirtysomething at thirty: an oral history* was published by Bear Manor Media. After years of wishing and hoping, I was an author with a major release. Now, I can see how you might be at home saying, "Well you had interviews from Emmy-winning actors. Of course they took your book."

But that isn't what led to the sale. It was what happened a year before on Twitter that led to me selling the book.

The key factor for you to learn from this moment was I was open to that tweet from Richard Kramer. I was brave enough to ask for an interview. I prepared for the interview like I was Barbara Walters (Do people remember who she was? She was someone in my day), did a competent job with Richard Kramer, and that led me to the book. I am a writer of books about television solely because I had the nerve to ask for the interview. I wasn't thinking about a book at that moment. I was just trying to make the next step, any step. The reason I could get that interview was because I was the host of a podcast. The reason I impressed Richard Kramer in that interview was because I had studied television for years. I had thoughtful questions and didn't act like a novice. At that point in time, I didn't know writing about television would be what I would do for the foreseeable future. I was still hoping I was going to be a novelist or a screenwriter. It all happened because I was *open to the opportunity* and then backed it up with skill. I prepared for the moment of my first "real" book to be published in 2017 since 1981, when I wrote that first book as a pre-teen. Every moment in between prepped me.

My next project is probably the most on-point self-publishing story there can be. I was a huge fan of *Twin Peaks* when it aired on ABC in 1990. In 2017, it returned to television for a new season that aired on Showtime. I knew from my *Red Room Podcast*, named after *Twin Peaks*, there were a ton of rabid *Peaks* fans. I knew there was going to be interest and plenty of clues to decipher. I wanted there to be a magazine that covered the show. So If I wanted it, why don't I start it? Why couldn't I do it? There was no reason. All I had to do was find writers to help me write it, find a printer who could print a full-color magazine, learn how to design a magazine, figure out how to build a website to sell it, be sure that Showtime wouldn't sue me, find interviews from the actors from the series, and get a couple of thousand people to buy it. What could be easier?

I contacted a few *Twin Peaks* scholars who I was certain could write great essays about the series. They were all willing to join. I started Twitter and Facebook accounts called *The Blue Rose* (a mysterious plot point from the series) and started posting ominous posts that something from *Twin Peaks* was coming. I created a music video on YouTube which never mentioned what *The Blue Rose* was, but said it was coming. The *Twin Peaks* online community started posting and speculating what it could be. Someone even posted how this "Blue Rose" thing must be from Showtime because the quality of the promo videos were so high. I was creating buzz and intrigue before having written a single word.

In the meantime, I had to learn how to publish a magazine and list an eBook on Amazon. I wanted the first issue to come out on February 24th, which is considered *Twin Peaks* day, due to a plot point from the series. I figured starting with the eBook was going to be a lot simpler than finding a printer and learning InDesign. At this point, I had never put a book together. Bear Manor designed my *thirtysomething* book for me. I bought a website (bluerosemag.com) and learned how to list products. That sentence really doesn't cover it. It was incredibly challenging for me to learn how to build that website and figure all of that out. It took weeks and was honestly one of the most unfun things I have ever done (and I was a stay-at-home dad with twins). I am not technologically brilliant like Erin is. It was a struggle, but through YouTube videos and help from friends, I got it done. I point this out to let you know that you may have to learn something that is not your strong suit, but that is all part of the job. Also, I have had a ton of people tell me how horrible that website is, but it works, so shut it.

On the Amazon eBook listing I mentioned this website for readers who were interested in buying the hardcopy of the magazine. Remember, this is a magazine that wasn't written, didn't exist yet, wasn't coming out for 3 months, and I had no idea how to print a hard copy. But who cared? I wasn't promoting it yet. I was just trying to learn how to list things. So who would ever know? Well, there was a diehard *Twin Peaks* fan who must have had an Amazon or Google alert set up to let them know whenever a new *Twin Peaks* product was listed. This person, who just happened to have over 38,000 followers, tweeted out the link to the hardcopy sale of Issue #1. My phone started to blow up. People were ordering Issue #1. I immediately panicked. I hadn't even tested if the PayPal link worked. I immediately logged in and, sure enough, there was a deposit of $10.99 in my account. And then another one. And another one. I had forty orders in over three hours. Forty orders for a magazine that didn't exist. I now had less than 3 months to create it all.

That was the most exciting day of my writing career and the closest to viral I've ever gotten. (Unless you count that one time in college.) I went from having an idea to potentially committing fraud on unsuspecting consumers. There is nothing like the idea of "jail time" to motivate you to learn. I started calling local printers in Columbus, Ohio to find someone who could make what I wanted. I found one and created a price plan that would work. On February 24, 2017, Issue #1 was released on Kindle and a hard copy was mailed out to 450 readers across the globe. As of 2021, we have published 15 issues, sold over 25,000 hard copies and plenty of Kindle editions on every continent. Showtime ended up sending us free promo cards for the new season to send out with our second issue. The show's creators would retweet our links, and most of the cast was open to being interviewed by the only magazine that covered the show. We never made it into brick and mortar bookstores, but we could at least sell enough to pay for the printing costs and stay in business.

Often authors are so focused on getting into Barnes & Noble or being for sale in airports. The point is, can you come up with a business plan to pay for printing and make a little extra? If I had tried to print 10,000 copies of this magazine, it would have folded early. We hit a high of 2,500 copies per issue the first year, and by 2021 we are only printing around 1,000. It is about adapting to shipping, printing and overhead costs. If you are going to self-publish, it's up to you to be the artist and the businessperson. This wasn't print on demand (POD). I was purchasing outright the amount and then hoping sales covered it. This can be an option for you if you are certain you can sell all you print and have the capital to front the printing costs. Because of the preorder sales over those three months, I didn't have to ever put my own money up to print the magazine. The advantages were that the printing quality was very high, and we got the lowest per issue price. (It is cheaper per issue to print 2,500 over 1 at a time.) Readers grew to expect that level of quality and would never accept a drop in the future. That meant that we could never go to POD. So we either have to continue to sell enough to print over 1,000 copies or quit.

The Blue Rose magazine is the ultimate in self-publishing. A singular idea, achieved all within the basement of my house, and sent out across the globe. The Kindle editions of the magazine have hit #1 a few times in the television category, which is incredible for an independent publisher. But I didn't stop there.

While running *The Blue Rose*, I made another Twitter connection. This time with Barbara Gaines, executive producer of *The Late Show with David Letterman*. The same thing that happened with *thirtysomething*, amazingly happened with my TV-best friend, David Letterman. I interviewed the entire writing staff and producers of the series. I had another book ready to go. Bear Manor Media would have published it in a second, but after designing *The Blue Rose* and marketing it myself, I decided I wanted to do this one on my own. I partnered with David Bushman, author of the *Twin Peaks FAQ* and *Buffy FAQ*, and we opened our own publishing company called Fayetteville Mafia Press. *The Last Days of Letterman* was our first book released through our company.

We weren't looking at this company as a self-publisher. We wanted our books to be in bookstores and have a real distributor. We started pitching our company to big distributors like Ingram and Baker & Taylor. They were all interested when we said our first book would have an inside look at the final six weeks of David Letterman's late-night career, but they asked us what else we had. We had nothing. The distributors we talked to wanted at least ten books a year and an agreement that we could bring in a quarter of a million dollars in sales a year. We would be lucky to make a quarter, let alone a quarter of a million. How could a new company start off with ten books? The system was created to stop new companies from springing up. I said to them, "But this Letterman book is a really great book and a wonderful start. No one has ever had this access before." I will never forget when the Ingram sales person said to me, "We don't care what's in the book; we care how much we can sell."

That is the rule of publishing. They don't care if the book is actually good. They don't even care if they can sell that book. Can they sell a bunch of books and make even more money? The publishing industry is a monopoly like every industry in America. So they have no interest in providing readers with one great book. The profit from one book is irrelevant to them. We kept looking. We ended up finding a mom-and-pop distributor who's owner loved Letterman and wanted to distribute the book. We signed with Midpoint Trade Books and three months after

The Last Days of Letterman was released, they were eaten by the largest independent distributor in the country, IPG. This meant that Fayetteville Mafia Press was now part of a huge distributor, and our books would be available everywhere. We are now releasing four books a year including *The Women of Amy Sherman-Palladino, Laura's Ghost: Women Speak about Twin Peaks, The Massillon Tigers: 15 for 15, Conversations with Mark Frost, Flight 7 is Missing: The Search for my Father's Killer*, and *Cracking The Wire During Black Lives Matter*.

I design the books and some of the covers. I do most of the marketing on our social media accounts and have learned a ton over the past five years. My partner edits the books and works on getting reviews. I have experience with self-publishing, working through a traditional publisher, and being a publisher. Through these pages I will share stories on why I suggest that you do certain things. In writing this summary of the last few years, the through line is this: Each person and experience I encountered, I learned from it and made sure I wasn't stagnant. I linked myself with smart, talented people and grew from the relationships. I never said, "No." I was open, professional, and aware of every opportunity. You have to be ready to be uncomfortable and do things you don't want to do. I had to learn how to run these businesses while I was writing for the magazine and writing my books. You will have to wear more than one hat. And I bet, that like me, you only have one head.

Chapter Takeaways

1. You will have to be an artist and a businessperson.

2. Having a podcast or a large social media presence helps with creating buzz and sales.

3. You can print your own book and do it all yourself with no distributor, IF your project has a built in fan base.

CHAPTER THREE

How Do I Develop a Story?

We have to assume that if you are here and interested in publishing, then you already have an idea for a book. Hopefully, this means you have already started to write. But in case you haven't, let's talk about content development. An idea sets you on the path. Advice from Broadway legend Stephen Sondheim is always helpful. He says content dictates form. So your idea sparks how you will go about achieving the end result. If you are writing a children's book, you are going to need art that engages a child. If you are doing a deep dive critical analysis of *Hamlet*, you probably aren't going to need a lot of flashy art. The overall idea behind the book is the building block for bringing it to life.

The first question you have to answer is: What is your goal for your book? Do you want to print a book you wrote when you were seven for your grandma? Or, do you have a great idea that you think could be the next best seller for the world? In some ways, the steps will be the same. You still need to write, design, and print it. But grandma is probably not going to care as much about your margins, fonts or comma placement as a brick-and-mortar bookstore. Our goal for you is to create a book that has the same professional look as Stephen King's latest book. You want your book and his to sit side by side on the book shelf and look just as good. (Of course your last name would also have to start with "K" for that to happen, but whatever.)

Self-publishing may be free from the confines of publishing house expectations, but that doesn't mean there aren't still standards to abide by. It will be your name that is associated with this project. So, be rough on yourself. Set high standards. Writing is thankless, hard work. It should be a struggle. Or, at least, the final draft should be. Editing and restructuring can be a nightmare. You don't have any other choice but to just do it. Every idea that turned into one of our projects wasn't because we wanted to do it. It was because we didn't have a choice. The idea beat out our desire to sit down and watch *Friends* reruns. We had a story to tell, ideas to share, and we simply couldn't rest until we had word vomited onto the page. Then, much later, edited the crap out of it.

So, where do ideas come from and how do you know if it's a good one? Most of this will be a result of intuition. Some of it may be market research and demand. No matter what, ask yourself what many traditional publishers would typically ask if you were to submit a proposal: What gives you the authority to write this book? If it's a personal narrative, the answer should be a no-brainer. If it's an in-depth analysis based in theoretical quantum physics, you should probably have read more than one scientific article. The best rule of thumb is to write what you know. Even if you have to do a little research, start with where you're most comfortable and develop additional content from there. Most of all, let your world guide you. Brilliant ideas are around every corner; you just have to be paying attention long enough to catch them.

•••••

Scott: The first book that I published was an eBook only. I had been telling comic short stories about my crazy life at dinner parties, at work, in the line at the grocery store, everywhere and anywhere. Telling short funny stories was what I did best. In 2012, I started a podcast called *Scott Luck Stories* where I recorded those stories in five to seven minute episodes. (I don't have good luck. I don't have bad luck. I have Scott Luck. [Want to know what Scott Luck is? Head on out to Amazon and find out. Note, that is how an author is always marketing]) In 2014 when I had about twenty-five episodes, I thought it was time to compile them into a book. Basically my idea was to take me and shove me into an eBook and sell it for $.99. I think the last time I checked I had only sold about 100 downloads over six years. But if there is one thing that I will repeat over and over in this book, it's that you don't do these things for money. If you want to be rich, be born into it. If you want to create, be an artist. Create art and let the money fall where it may…which will be into the hands of people who already have it. What I got out of *Scott Luck Stories* was that I had published a book on my own.

The point for you is that my idea for my first book came out of what I was good at in that moment of my life. I was making people laugh with my stories of running the drive-thru at Arby's or my time as a stay-at-home dad.

Keys to a Strong Idea

What is your strong suit as a writer?

What are you best at?

What experience have you had that others might not have?

What do you want to share with the world?

This, by no means, is the finish line. You might be passionate about cooking, but if you don't know how to deconstruct a dish into a recipe, then doing a cookbook is probably not for you. It's a mix of many factors that you must bring to a book. It has to be something that only you can do. What can you create with your unique perspective or opinion?

•••••

Erin: From the *Babysitter's Chronicles* drafted at a corner desk in a second grade classroom to an intense poem about a tree, the artistry of words has always been part of my identity. It is when I'm lying awake late at night when unique phrases and illustrative thoughts come flooding into my brain; thoughts that eventually make their way into blog posts, articles, or even poetry. It will start with a few key words or even a rhythm, and when the sentences begin to pile up, I know there is a solid idea holding it all together. Whenever I sit down to write, I always start there. I start from the core of the story.

My writing process for *Gui Ren* began with re-reading my blog posts, filling in some illustrative details that weren't as critical in short-form storytelling, and connecting the bite-sized stories with additional context. The drive behind my idea was to bring readers into my international adventures and communicate the power of synchronicity and kindness. Because of the nature of my adventures in Asia, I had a clear point A to point B to point C, but not every manuscript is compiled that way. Your story may not be linear, but if it holds a powerful idea within its grips, then the rest will develop in time. Trust it. Follow it. Give it the chance to turn into something more.

Pay attention to the world around you. What resonates with you and your understanding of the world? What intrigues or excites you? Take note of the conversations that spark your creativity. If you feel inspired to write, do it. If it's calling you, poking at your brain, egging you on to sit down and process, follow the instinct. Consider why it's important to you, how it has shaped you as an individual, or why you feel driven to connect with others through the marriage. There's something in that particular idea that is calling to you, and the only way to figure out what that might be is to process it. Fall into it with your whole heart.

Use Your Resources

Artistic perception and creation is unique to every individual, but we are often influenced by other creators and producers in our world. Creative minds inspire and challenge one another continuously. We often find ourselves moved to respond to art in our own ways. If you've ever been at a concert and started to dance, you know what we're talking about. Art influences art; authors inspire authors. Everything you do is likely encouraged or supported by another creative mind at work. We challenge you to see this as a tool and harness its power to establish your own path.

To be clear, we're not advocating for copyright infringement. No, no, no. Not cool. What we are encouraging is the use of resources. This means doing your homework. Pick up a few of your favorite books. Study the structure of their narratives, compare literary voices, reference their cover designs, and take a careful look at formatting. Without even reading a "How To" guide, you can begin to develop an understanding of the logistics and technical elements of publishing a book.

Storytelling

Once you have an idea, whether it be fiction, non-fiction, or fairytale, you'll need to develop the story in a way that allows the reader to process a narrative without getting lost along the way. Telling a good story is more involved than picking a character and placing them in a particular environment. If writing an impactful narrative were that simple, we'd still be listening to Mrs. Nancy's first grade class recite stories about a dog named Frank. So, when it comes time to start writing your manuscript, there are a few methods you could use to further narrow down your story.

•••••

Erin: There's a reason there are entire master class series about storytelling; it's an art form with the power to influence perspectives and craft a narrative that continuously feeds into itself. It's an everyday tool that we use in casual conversations, yet the most talented of tellers often need several years of focused development to be considered a skillful performer. Even natural-born storytellers spend decades refining their abilities. I fell into storytelling after years of theatre, reading, and writing. And I fell into it by accident.

When I came home from Asia, I began sharing my experiences with others—bringing them into my world and illustrating the life-changing interactions I collected on my journey. At the time, it was a casual conversation, but then someone suggested I take it to a stage. So, I attended a storytelling event at my local library and found the courage to give it a try. I stepped onto a stage with a crinkled outline in hand, ready to recall my journey into the jungle with a stranger I had met on a beach. I started off by apologizing to the audience for needing my notes at the ready. I proceeded to attempt to remember every detail as I recited my script. Although I had the audience's attention from the first line, "My mom always told me not to talk to strangers..." I didn't fully capture their hearts until closer to the end, when I set my script aside and retold the story from the heart. I learned a very important lesson that day. Live storytelling isn't about memorizing a perfectly written piece; it's about reliving a moment in time and bringing listeners into that space with you. Storytelling in the performance space is recreating an experience for a live audience.

Of course, a good story still requires basic understanding of what makes an engaging narrative. Whether in casual conversation or standing on a stage, telling an impactful story can take practice. My personal genre of storytelling is what I would consider to be transformative storytelling; I take a moment in time and illustrate how the series of events shifted my perspective or changed an aspect of my life. To do this effectively I need to first establish where I was, what I went through, and then how it altered my human experience moving forward. This is just one of many approaches or techniques used in storytelling.

•••••

Most are familiar with the hero's journey (see *The Wizard of Oz*), a common structure that is often found in folktales and myths. Some utilize a mountain method when composing their narratives which slowly builds suspense and drama before delivering a satisfying conclusion (see *Rocky*). *In medias res* is a familiar structure particular to TV shows and movies in which the audience begins in the middle of a story only to then return to the beginning and travel through the remainder of the narrative for full context (see almost every episode of *The West Wing*). The false start structure is another unique way to engage audiences with an establishment of trust that is later revealed to be a false sense of security. Whichever technique you select, developing the plot with intent every step of the way can make the difference between a captivating or snooze-worthy story.

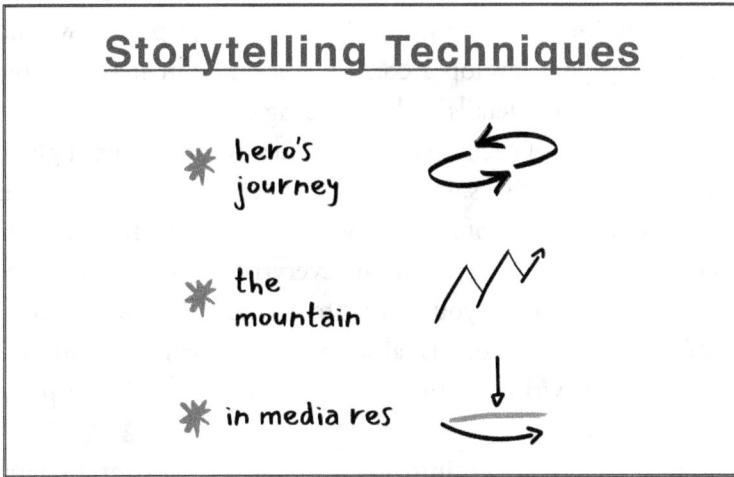

Storytelling Techniques

* hero's journey
* the mountain
* in media res

In addition to selecting the structure that best reflects your narrative goals, storytellers can craft their story in a variety of different tones and include unique elements that make their piece stand out. Some tellers lean into comedy while others are grounded in a more serious tone. My own voice tends to be casual and light-hearted but with built-in opportunity for deeper connection and analytical reflection. Finding a voice that works for you is critical in delivering a meaningful and purposeful story. Even in written form, a voice comes through, so make sure to spend the time to ensure it's the right one. Take note of the stories or literary voices that you most resonate with and look for commonalities in your writing style. This can help you determine a starting point for your own voice, a voice that will continue to develop in the creative process.

If you are struggling to develop your voice or identify the most captivating elements of your story, here are a few techniques to try:

- Tell the story in a variety of ways, under a variety of time constraints. Set a timer and only allow yourself ten minutes to write it all down; perform it for a friend but only give yourself five minutes; record yourself and listen for the moments in which you were truly invested in the details. Oftentimes it is the most critical elements of your narrative that will be consistent across all recordings. Those are the details on which to build your story.

- Compose the story through the eyes of another character, in either fiction or nonfiction. Taking a new perspective will not only help you develop a concise storyline but may also pull out unexpected details and describing elements.

- Hire a ghostwriter. Not everyone is adept enough to write a book; that's just the cold hard truth. And there's a reason even professional writers use proofreaders and editors. No one is good at everything, so don't expect that just because you want to write a book you'll be able to do it. There is absolutely no shame in hiring a professional writer to bring your story to life on the pages.

Taking an idea and turning it into an engaging and captivating narrative can take time, skill, and an insurmountable number of drafts. Storytelling is a developed skill that requires dedication and practice to be a truly effective method of communicating experiences and perspectives. Having a solid idea is just the beginning step to the journey to self-publishing. Make sure to invest energy into the narrative and breathe life into the details. If you have an idea worth sharing, make sure it develops into a story worth telling.

•••••

Scott: All of my work has been nonfiction, but that doesn't mean it is not steeped in storytelling. No matter what your book is about, you have to be sure your reader understands what you are saying. Be clear, start at the beginning, use the proper language that matches your content, and always stay on point. The secret to a good storyteller is their ability to keep the reader engaged. Be respectful of your reader's time. Edit out the chum.

Most of the challenges a self-publisher has to deal with are unfortunately not about writing. Along with writing your spectacular manuscript, you have to design, market, promote, and launch your book. But none of that will matter if the words weren't worth all that energy. The fundamental basis of all writing is the story you have to tell.

To start, plan out the path of your book. When I did my book on the TV series *thirtysomething*, I decided I would split the book up between the eighty-five episodes of the series. That meant the book had eighty-five chapters because I was covering every episode. This let me keep track of the story. When I conducted each interview, I would split up their comments by episode. It made it a lot easier for me. But a book that has eighty-five chapters, with some being just one page, gets kind of annoying. The reason I made this annoying choice was because I wanted people to be able to watch the series as they read the book. In my opening introduction essay, I explained the thought process of how I structured the book according to episodes that served as a guide for those reading and watching along. When I created my book on the TV Series *Moonlighting*, the book was more about the overall creative process, so the book was split up into chapters that covered different topics. I still told the story in chronological order, but it was based more on the tensions that were rising as each season of the show progressed. Both of these concepts were something I came up with BEFORE I started writing. This is, in fact, an example of storytelling. I had to figure out what is the best way to communicate the information in the most consumable way.

The *Moonlighting* book starts out with a nostalgic feel as Bruce Willis and Cybill Shepherd are cast in the series. Because I had done all the interviews and research before I started writing, I do not let the reader know that in the middle of the book all hell is going to break loose, and the book is going to get anything but nostalgic. I want the reader to experience it as it actually unfolded. I want the book to read like a story even though it really happened. So the reader starts out with nostalgia, moves to drama, and then comes back around to the legacy and lifelong friendships the show created among the crew. As an artist, I love how readers will be surprised about what happens in the last half of the book. It will be a shock. As a businessman, I want to put a note in there that says, "Keep reading, I promise you it is gonna get crazy later." But that is the worst kind of storytelling because if I tip my hand, I will take the journey away from the reader. All I can do is trust they will take the bait. So, even in a nonfiction book, I am leading my readers through the dramatic progress of a fiction book.

Even though both books told stories of a TV show, they each had a different story to tell and a different way I chose to tell each story. I used my skills as a storyteller and screenwriter to give the reader the best experience. I adapted the concept that made the most sense and matched that with the material I had. You can try to force your book to be what you want, but it won't be any good. Let the book be what it wants to be. Tell the story the way the story wants to be told.

Picking a Title

Hopefully, your title will come to you in the process of developing your manuscript, if it is not the very first decision you make. A title has a few functions. It will prepare the reader for what is in store and might indicate the theme or purpose of your work. In the days of social media, a title might also become the trending hashtag in your marketing efforts.

•••••

Erin: There were many reasons I decided on self-publishing, but one of the primary factors was my title. As I was traveling through Southeast Asia, I continued meeting people who changed my perspective or redirected my life's course. As I was explaining this unexpected phenomena of continued life-changing interactions, my Singaporean friend, Augustine, pointed out that I am experiencing Gui Ren. Gui Ren is a written Chinese phrase that encompasses the people who enter our lives with synchronicity to help guide or inspire us when we least expect it. As soon as she shared this term with me, I knew I finally had words that described the relationships that had been a critical aspect of my personal development over the previous several months. She had finally put into two simple words what I couldn't seem to find.

When I decided to turn my blog posts into a book, I could think of no better title than *Gui Ren*. It was the defining characteristics of every story and served as an homage to the culture and language in which I was so deeply immersed. In honoring my story and my authentic self, however, I would be opting for a title that wasn't in English. Non-English titles aren't necessarily a problem, but depending on the cover design and associated marketing, it can certainly detract American consumers from reaching beyond the front page. I would have understood if a traditional publisher insisted I change it. So, I didn't even give them a chance to make the request. It was *Gui Ren*, or it wasn't my story.

•••••

Scott: When I was preparing the *Twin Peaks* magazine, we had several titles to choose from, as *Twin Peaks* is a very visual show with a ton of iconic moments. The problem was, in the twenty-five years since it aired, just about everything had been taken. My partners and I settled on the title of *Between Two Worlds*, which was a line of dialogue from the series. It also would set up the magazine coming out before the new series. It would bridge the two worlds of *Twin Peaks*—the original series and the new one.

Here is a great tip. Before you put your title in cement, do a Google, Amazon, Twitter, Go Daddy, Instagram, and Facebook search for the title. I did this kind of search while we were finalizing the title. There were no books out there about *Twin Peaks* with that title. The day before I was going to buy betweentwoworlds.com, I did one final search. That day, someone announced a book about *Twin Peaks* called *Between Two Worlds*. We were back to the drawing board. We later came up with *The Blue Rose* and luckily there was nothing under that name. You may ask, why not just call it the *Twin Peaks* magazine? Well, because CBS, which owns the series, could have sued us. In addition to originality, you want to be really careful with copyright laws. Any true *Twin Peaks* fan who hears *The Blue Rose* will, in their mind, link it with *Twin Peaks*, but we can't be sued for what happens in readers' minds. (Thank goodness, because otherwise I'd be sued all the time.) Here are some of the covers we have done for *The Blue Rose*.

If you want to call your book *The Story*, for example, be sure you take the time to do a little research. A quick trip to Google lets you know that folk singer Brandi Carlile has a hit song and record under that name. Therefore, every time someone uses the hashtag #TheStory they are going to be talking about her, not you. You also want to check GoDaddy, a site where you can buy website domains to see if you can get your title for a dot com. This will make it easier to tell people where they can buy your book, and they won't forget the URL when they encourage others to buy it, too. When I was publishing the book *The Massillon Tigers: 15 for 15*. We couldn't get 15for15.com but we could get 15for15book.com.

On the creative side, make sure your title lets readers know what they are in store for. Let's say you are writing a book about improving the reader's memories. You might not want to call the book *I Can't Remember the Name of the Book* because that is counter intuitive to people talking about your book. They will tell their friends, "I just read this great book that has really helped me with my memory." The friend will ask, "What's it called?" And they will respond, "*I Can't Remember the Name of the Book*." Now, it makes a great Abbott and Costello bit, but not a great book title. Bad idea aside, it's also quite a long title. Will it fit on the cover? Will potential readers be able to digest the title as they scroll past it on Amazon looking for books to improve their memory? Of course, they may not remember any of the titles because they haven't read the book yet.

Chapter Takeaways

1. You must start your project with a strong idea and stay the course.

2. Storytelling is the key to all books, fiction or nonfiction. Your reader deserves a good story.

3. Pick a title that sets expectations and be sure it isn't already used.

CHAPTER FOUR

Why Self-Publishing?

Agent vs. Agency: How do you decide between hiring an agent or using agency and doing your own thing? Let's be honest, you might not have a choice of which publishing path you follow. It is notoriously difficult to convince a publishing company to buy an idea from an author. You may send your proposal to a number of agencies and be rejected from every single one. It could be the development of your idea, your writing style, financial considerations, or the genre that disinterested them. Either way, the great thing about today's world of publishing is that now you have another route to take. While it may be worthwhile to at least give publishing houses a try, if all else fails, there's another avenue for getting your work out into the world: Publish the book yourself. But for the purpose of this discussion, let's pretend you have the luxury of deciding between self-publishing and working with an agency.

We want to be sure that we are clear that there is nothing wrong with either choice, traditional or self. Scott runs a traditional publishing company with FMP, so obviously we believe there are clear advantages to that avenue. It really, at this point, is the only way to get your book in bookstores worldwide. Bookstores don't want to deal with a bunch of different suppliers. They want to deal with Ingram, which supplies books to brick and mortar stores. Is it a monopoly? Yes. Aren't they illegal in America? Only on paper. We want you to choose whichever path works best for you. In the Appendix of this book we have asked different authors to tell you which path they chose and why. There is no right answer. We are focusing more on the self side because we figure that is probably what you want to learn if you bought this book.

Whether you're an author, publisher, or reader, you likely know a few key differences between traditional and self-publishing without having to turn to Google. Some of these may be accurate assumptions while others might require a deeper look into the potential challenges or benefits. We'll cover some of the major considerations that should be part of your decision-making process.

Professionalism: The appearance of your printed book can have a significant impact on how quickly or widespread it sells. We'll talk more later on about formatting and standard publication practices, but whether you're a first time author or bestseller, there are certain expectations you should follow in order to be taken seriously. Working with a traditional publisher, especially a well-known agency, will ensure that your book meets those standards. Self-publishing will require more energy on your part to make sure your book can sit side-by-side with Stephen King's and not look terribly out of place. If you don't have the skill set or interest in making your book look professional, you may want to consider traditional publishing or farm out the design section to the professionals at Fishtail Publishing.

Prestige: Let's be honest, telling your family you published your own book on Amazon does sound a little less impressive than, "Harper Collins just sent an advance for my manuscript!" Self-publishing doesn't have the same kind of prestige as traditional. That being said, there is an alternative kind of prestige in self-publishing. Maybe you would take more pride in completing a DIY project than having your work validated by a major publisher. If that sounds like you, self-publishing might be the way to go. But also remember "prestige" isn't free. It comes with a hand in your pocket. A company like Harper Collins has a lot of board members to feed, and they will be taking a share of your profit. Everything is a balance.

Speed of Production: Traditional publishing can take an excessive amount of time from the moment you begin submitting book proposals to contacting literary agents. Writing query letters and contacting agents consumes quite a bit of time, especially if you're taking the submission process seriously. You should be researching each agent's previous publication lists, preferences, and working in some personal connections in your query. After sending those off to the agents, you have to wait. And wait. And probably wait some more. It could take months to hear back from agents, years to finally land one, and more time to sign a publishing contract. Any publisher worth their wait is going to have a time table stretching out for a few years, so once you get that traditional publisher, they are not going to want to publish your book for at least 18 months-36 months, depending on their timeline. With self-publishing, you can list your book for sale as soon as Amazon's 72-hour review period is complete.

Creative Control: This will vary depending on the contract you sign and what decisions you retain the ability to influence. However, it is not uncommon for traditional publishers to require that certain elements become their jurisdiction as soon as you sign your name on the dotted line. The cover design, title, or marketing tactics for your book may no longer be yours to control, which means you may end up with a final product that doesn't fully fulfill your expectations. Additionally, you may be assigned to an editor who suggests content changes that are less than ideal. These can occasionally be minor inconveniences in traditional publishing, or they could leave you wishing you had maintained control over your work. If you know you want full control, self-publishing would be a better path to take. But always be sure to listen to the experts, just because they don't tell you what you want to hear, doesn't mean they are wrong.

Distribution: One of the major benefits to a traditional publisher is distribution. Getting your book into brick and mortar stores is far easier with a traditional publisher. This is, arguably, the number one reason to go with a traditional publisher, if you are already leaning that direction. Self-publishing leaves this work to the author, but can be made easier through specific channels. We will cover more of this later.

Marketing: Depending on how much is invested in the publication, many publishers offer or provide marketing agents to assist with the launch of your title. They are also the ones to promote your work to brick and mortar bookstores. While this can be a benefit for many authors who prefer to be completely hands off with marketing efforts, in the age of social media it has become increasingly easy to reach consumers with your products. There are also some major review companies, like *Publisher's Weekly*, who will only review books that come from a traditional, established company. Even independent publishers like FMP can't break into that elite club. Self-publishing authors are hardly left out to dry without the assistance of a marketing agent. With platforms like Instagram, Facebook, Twitter, and even TikTok, it's possible to reach your audiences regardless of whether you pay someone else to do it for you. Traditional publishers have a ton of books to promote, so their focus will be pulled to those with the greatest chance of bringing home dollars and on the authors who invest the most in their marketing assistance. Unless you sign up for the gold package, most publishers will still rely on you to market your book. That is why they asked you how many followers you have before they ask you to sign your contract.

Royalties and Fees: This, too, depends on the contract you sign. With a traditional publisher you are much more likely to receive an advance for the completion of your book. The royalty rate will also vary depending on the agreement between you and the publisher. Further, royalty rates can vary depending on the self-publishing channel you choose. So, we can't provide a clear expectation for you when it comes to royalties. What we can tell you is that, if a publisher requires you to pay upfront for a publishing deal, this is more likely a vanity publisher, and you should be very cautious when reviewing any contracts. Vanity presses offer bundled services that include proofreading, cover designs, book design, and more. Make sure your sales will cover that cost and that you can eventually break even by selling copies on your own.

We hate to do this to you, but we are going to do some math in a hypothetical traditional publishing deal. Somehow the market place decided that wholesaling was a good idea. This means if your book has a list price of $25, the publisher sells it to the bookstore for $12.50.

Right away, the end seller is going to get more money than you will because you are sharing that $12.50 with the publisher. Let's say you sign a contract for 10% royalties of the $12.50. You would have to sell a lot of books and add up a lot of $1.20s to make a reasonable amount of money. If you self-publish, Amazon is going to take 50% at a minimum, but at least you get to keep the other 50%.

Literary Award Qualification: There are many literary prizes for which authors who wander down the path of self-publishing would not qualify. However, with the increasing presence of self-published authors there have emerged many other awards or recognitions you can explore. It may just take a little more research to find them.

Contracts: Obviously, with self-publishing, there is no contract beyond agreeing to your publishing channel's terms and conditions or if you decide to hire a contractor to assist with production. With traditional publishing, there should always be a contract, and you should always take reviewing this document seriously. As with any contract, take the time to review the terms and read the fine print. You will thank yourself later for being informed and prepared.

Editors are a Must

You may notice we didn't spend any time discussing the editing process. That is because there is no choice. Get an editor. Traditional publishing or not, this is essential to your success. You can't edit your own work. You need another person to have fresh eyes on your book. There is no discussion. Everyone needs an editor. Even if you use a service like Grammarly to do a first round of grammatical edits, premium paid subscription or not, you need a human who can perceive your work from the mind of an everyday reader. Even this sentence would benefit from editing. I am sure it was worse before our editor, the wonderful Courtenay Stallings, got at it. (*Hey, we didn't call her wonderful. Courtenay added that.*) A friend can give you advice. They can be great first readers, but an editor knows the rules and has a skill that most friends don't have. It really will make a huge difference.

<u>Words of Wisdom on Traditional Publishing</u>

Traditional publishing has it's benefits, as you've seen, but traditional publishers are book factories. There's nothing wrong with that, it's just the nature of their business model. They have many titles to manage at any given time and disperse their efforts accordingly. The reason they became a factory is because they had success. That success can help your book reach heights that you won't be able to attain by yourself. The fix is definitely in for the small author. At the end of the day, they are going to write contracts and establish working relationships in their favor. That's how for-profit businesses operate. This is not to say that your work is not valuable, it just means you are one of many writers competing for a similar slot. If you decide to pursue traditional publishing, you should go all in. And we're not talking hot dog eating competition all in, we're talking big league, international beauty contest judged by the largest fashion icons of the century. Tension. Is. High. All of this has a role to play in the decision you make about your published work. Whichever decision you make, decide with confidence and forge ahead. And, there's no reason you can't first make an attempt at traditional publishing but turn to self-publishing if your work isn't attracting enough interest. Whatever you do, commit to it.

•••••

Erin: If my closest friends could tell you anything about me (besides the good stuff, of course) they might tell you that I am quite an impatient person. When I began writing *Gui Ren*, I had the dream of working with a traditional publisher. I hoped they might drool over the adventurous stories and beg me to sign with them. I would start an all-out war between agents. I soon realized, however, that the time and energy required for submitting a nonfiction book proposal to agents all over the country was not as advantageous as I first assumed. There were ultimately three reasons I strayed from traditional publishing.

First and foremost, especially in the nonfiction arena, the materials required to submit a query can be daunting. Not only did I need to write the book, I would have to then summarize each chapter and provide a reason as to why the stories would be enticing to target audiences. Unlike fiction queries, which can often be as simple as sending the first five to ten pages of your manuscript, nonfiction book proposals require validation of why you are the person to write the book. Drafting a letter explaining why I have the authority to tell my own story felt somewhat ridiculous. After spending my weekend in an Internet-devoid, distraction-free cabin cranking out my outline, I bailed on the whole thing. I finished the outline, wrote a query letter, and then never submitted either of them.

The process of submitting book proposals and waiting to hear back from publishers was not in my MO. I like my results to arrive yesterday. Plus, the stories I wanted to tell were itching to come alive, and people were anxiously waiting to hear them. I didn't have time to waste. Because I had shared blog posts during my journey through Southeast Asia, and gained enough of a following on Facebook, the question kept hitting my notification feed, "When do we get to read the book?" I managed to capture an audience and didn't want to lose them in the time it might take to finally find a publisher.

The final, and perhaps most important reason I went with self-publishing, was authenticity. I wanted to tell my story the way it felt most natural. I feared the day someone might tell me to cut a character or omit a story because it didn't have enough of a selling point. Even small adjustments to make the book more appealing to readers would minimize the authenticity of my work. I didn't care about appeal, I cared about telling the story truthfully. Additionally, the title of my book is not in English, which I feared would negatively impact the chances of a traditional publisher picking up the manuscript. The title, as I shared with you earlier, was non-negotiable since it was central to the overall purpose for which the book was written.

Ultimately, I chose self-publishing because I wanted full ownership over my story, and I wanted it to be available for readers within the year after I returned from my trip. I didn't mind the challenge of having to design the interior or produce cover art. In fact, I happily accepted the challenge of putting more work on my plate. I found it interesting to dive into the world of publishing and learn all that I could about how to professionally produce a print book. Sure enough, that tedious research has served me ever since, as I now assist others in self-publishing their work.

SELF-PUBLISHING

CREATIVE CONTROL

- Maintain full creative control
- Hire your own team of professionals including designers and editors

SPEED OF PRODUCTION

- With a finished manuscript, you can have a book available for print-on-demand within 72 hours
- The process is entirely dependent on your investment and preferences

ROYALTIES AND FEES

- Royalties are usually higher, although you may not sell as many copies
- Ordering author copies and selling through your own channels increases income

MARKETING & DISTRIBUTION

- In today's world of social media, it has become even easier to reach readers around the world
- Determine and manage your own distribution methods; personalize the purchasing experience

PRESTIGE

- Self-publishers create their own prestige
- Although your title may not be aligned with a major publishing company, the pride and accomplishment can be in doing it on your own

PROFESSIONALISM

- Obtaining professionalism in a self-published work requires more attention to detail
- Reference previously published works for guidance on margins, image use, cover layout, and page distribution

TRADITIONAL PUBLISHING

CREATIVE CONTROL

- Often requires control over certain elements of the publication, particularly for marketing purposes
- May not be able to hire your preferred editor or designers

SPEED OF PRODUCTION

- Can take years to finish the process
- Submitting book proposals and sample pages adds time and energy to your process
- Finding a literary agent is often more difficult than applying to jobs

ROYALTIES AND FEES

- More likely to receive an advance
- Royalties are lower due to the additional people who need to be paid

MARKETING & DISTRIBUTION

- Access to professional marketing and distribution channels
- May be required to sacrifice more royalties for these services
- Will likely sell more copies

PRESTIGE

- Professional affiliation and reputable publishing association
- More likely to be attractive to other publishing houses for future titles

PROFESSIONALISM

- Guaranteed professional appearance, particularly when working with a well-established agency
- Proper database categorization, ISBN, and barcode placement

•••••

Scott: One of my books was published through a traditional publisher. Bear Manor Media publishes a ton of television books, and I was sure they would work hard to get the word out to *thirtysomething* fans. I learned pretty quickly that was going to be my job. When they sent me the contract, it had a word count and a due date, but that was about all. I didn't get an advance, I didn't get a photo budget, and it was up to me to design the cover. They had an inhouse designer who put my book together, but it wasn't anything flashy, and it wasn't anything that displayed my personality. Yes, I was listed on their website. Yes, I was with a "real" publisher, but what does that mean? They print their books as print on demand, so Barnes & Noble and other brick and mortar stores won't carry *thirtysomething at thirty* because the book is unreturnable (we'll talk more later about what that means and why it's important). This would be the same case if I had published the book through Amazon's print on demand. So, what really was the difference?

One of the really great parts of having a publisher is not having to put up any money. When I go to print on an FMP book, I put all the capital up. I have to prepay for every issue of *The Blue Rose*. With *thirtysomething*, it only cost me time. Now, that also means I don't reap the financial benefits either. At the time, I didn't know how to design books, so I didn't have to worry about any of that. But, I didn't like their design at all.

However, the benefit of going with a publisher for my first book paid off when I started doing interviews for my follow up book about David Letterman. I could tell Letterman's producers I was a published author. I could send the link to the website, as well as send a copy of my book to them. It gave me a bit of clout that I had a book under my belt. Now, to be fair, I have no idea if that would have been any more or less convincing if I would have sent that same *thirtysomething* book under the Scott Ryan Productions logo. But, it was exciting to have those books arrive. It was unbearably exciting when I got that email that read "Sold." I even took a picture of me signing the contract for posterity sake. In the end, I still haven't made much money off that book. My goal when I was publishing the *thirtysomething* book was to make money, not gain status points. I was just about to be downsized from a job I hated, and I wanted to make money and be a writer. I was 46, and it was time.

In 2020, ABC announced *thirtysomething* was going to be rebooted. I was excited as I thought this would revive sales of my book. I contacted BMM and asked what marketing they would do to coincide with the premiere of the new season? They said none. I asked if we could get copies in bookstores for the release? They said no because the returns would be too high. If I had complete control over the book, I could have made these things happen. No fear, because in the end, COVID-19 killed the reboot and ABC passed (Scott Luck is always in play) so none of it happened, but there was still nothing I could do to control big decisions about the book because I didn't own it. All of these things might have been different with a huge publisher. I don't know. In the end, I decided I want to own what I do. If I am going to crash and burn, I want to be the one calling the shots. (Hey, what's that fire behind me? Oh, it's me crashing and burning.)

So, You've Decided to Stick with Self-Publishing

If you decide to go with traditional publishing, congratulations. If you decide that self-publishing will better meet your needs for ownership and efficiency, you need to be willing to go the distance. Self-publishing is a lot of work. Rewarding, sure, but it can be utterly exhausting. And, even when you have published a bookshelf worth of titles, you still won't get it done without errors. Talk to different people and they may all give you varying opinions on where the page numbers should be located and how large the cover font should be. But if you follow the standards and use previously published works as a reference guide, your book can still look professional. It is guaranteed that you will get something wrong on your first publication, but don't let that discourage you from continuing to use self-publishing as your foundation for sharing your narrative. Each book will be better than the last.

Self-publishing requires a certain amount of self discipline and determination. Without the strict deadlines of a publisher, it can be easy to fall behind on your goals and set the book down just long enough that it never gets picked back up. Additionally, it's much easier to fall prey to distractions and the daily grind of normal life. It was, in fact, in the middle of reviewing this manuscript when Erin received a text from her fiancé about the impeachment trials. She turned to Scott and said, "Oh, look, the impeachment voting has started." It was a perfect example of the sort of distractions that can prevent someone from finishing a manuscript. Although she hadn't intended to start a long, divergent conversation about politics or the state of the country, it could have easily turned into one. Instead, it turned into a conversation about how important it is to turn off notifications and remove any distractions from your writing space. Either way, Erin and Scott were instantly removed from the task at hand. So, do yourself a favor and set up a distraction-free writing zone. Set a schedule with an intention to write for even just twenty minutes a day. Know yourself and your work ethic, and set up a system that will help you finish your book efficiently and effectively. Your idea and your story will thank you.

<u>Choosing a Publishing Platform</u>

Print on demand refers to the process that takes place when a book is purchased. On Amazon, for example, they print a copy only when someone buys your book. A consumer demands it with their wallet, Amazon prints it right then and there. As the author, you are charged (and paid) for just that book and there is no expenditure of capital. Let's do some quick math. If your book is $9.99 and Amazon charges $2 to print it, you get $7.99 from the book. After Amazon takes their 40-70% of the profit, you are down to about $2.40 a book. However, you didn't put any money out, maintained complete control of the product, and didn't have to ship the book because Amazon took care of that for you.

Before we send you running to a mass publisher, remember what Scott did with *The Blue Rose*. If you know you can sell a certain amount (at least 500) you could always find a local printer to print your own books and sell them on your website, Ebay, list them as an Amazon seller, or make local appearances at bookstores in your area. If you're going to use a local printer, however, leave time for meaningful research into the reputation of the company and its success with publishing. You could use a printer like Blurb.com that simply compiles your manuscript and cover art and sends you boxes of printed copies. However, unless you want to invest additional royalties, they won't provide you a channel to promote and sell it. This would also require you to have capital, a built in market, and a lot of guts. That being said, if Scott did it, you can do it, too. (Note: Scott had the widespread popularity of a cult classic TV show on his side and seven years of hosting a podcast on the topic.)

But why would you risk printing 500 copies and putting up the capital, if you can just print one book on Amazon for less? The answer is simple: quality. If you have a ton of pictures, or if your book is in color, the difference of using a short run print over POD is huge. The quality is remarkable. If your book is in black and white and is text only, there honestly isn't much of a difference.

We are assuming, for the sake of the rest of this chapter, that you are going to use one of the big self-publishers. Three popular options for self-publishing authors are Amazon, BookBaby, and IngramSpark. All platforms are print on demand services that offer book assembly, production, and distribution, and have partnerships with just about every major bookstore in the United States. So, if you dream of seeing your title on the shelves of a local shop, both a short run print or print on demand would be reliable options. However, neither of these avenues have a designated sales force to help promote your title to book sellers. You will still need to approach these stores and put in a request to see your title, and it still isn't a guarantee that they'll put in an order.

The thing to know about getting your book into a store like Barnes & Noble (if they're even still around by the time you're reading this), is that most sellers require the title to be returnable. This means that if copies aren't selling or they have a surplus of returns, they need to be able to ship the title back. It makes sense to have this requirement, however, it comes at a cost. Most POD places don't want to take returns back because they have no place for them other than the garbage bin, so you just printed your book to throw it away. Unfortunately, this happens with print runs as well. It is the dark side of the publishing business. There is a huge environmental waste with the business model. Until the industry is pressured to care about the waste, the return process is going to continue. It really is a wash between POD or print runs, either way returns are going to be wasteful.

All that being said, self-publishing (especially without the assistance of an agent or publicist) is likely to result in a general disinterest from brick and mortar bookstores. If you choose this route of publication, it is unlikely that you will meander into a chain bookstore and be able to see your title on the shelf. If you do, it's probably because you invested additional resources beyond the basic self-publishing process. All the power to you, but we want you to go into this with an open mind.

•••••

Erin: I dreamed of seeing *Gui Ren* in bookstores and on the shelves of local libraries, but I ran as fast as I could from IngramSpark. For ten years I ran an annual book drive and giveaway for students in need. I combined my passion for reading and community service to help provide books for those who couldn't afford to have their own. I took unwanted books and gave them a new life with someone who needed them. So, when I began the process of uploading my manuscript to IngramSpark and was faced with one particular question, I bailed.

When it came time to decide whether or not I wanted my book to be returnable, I of course selected "yes." I wanted my title easily accessible to stores so that I had a chance of reaching new audiences. However, when IngramSpark then inquired about **how** I wanted to make my book returnable, I stared at the screen for several hours before closing the tab altogether.

My options were:

- Yes–Deliver: Your titles will be sold on a returnable basis. You will receive the physical copy of the returned book (this return option is only available for books sold in the United States or Canada). In addition to the wholesale cost of the book, shipping and handling fees will apply.
- Yes–Destroy: Your titles will be sold on a returnable basis. Returned units will be shipped back to Ingram and destroyed.

I was faced with two situations that were less than ideal. Either I would have to fund the return of copies that may or may be resellable, or perfectly good copies of my book would simply be destroyed. After ten years of donating my time and energy to repurposing books to prevent unreasonable waste in the interest of sharing the love of reading, destroying books was an absolute no-go for me. I was determined to find a way into bookstores without running myself low on funding or destroying works of literature.

Amazon KDP vs KDP Select vs Expanded Distribution

Amazon Kindle Direct Publishing (KDP) refers to the overall program that Amazon offers to allow you to publish both eBooks and paperbacks. It is what used to be CreateSpace before Amazon acquired the service and migrated all of the titles over to their platform. Without consideration of the additional bells and whistles (KDP Select or Expanded Distribution), Amazon KDP's basic service is to let authors upload eBooks and paperbacks for free. Authors are then issued royalties based on each copy sold.

Amazon KDP Select is an enrollment-based service for eBook publications only that offers a title for free to Kindle Unlimited subscribers. For $9.99 per month, Amazon customers can read as many books as they want to while subscribed to this program. With KDP Select, authors are paid by the pages read. It is important to know that, when you become part of the KDP Select program, you are agreeing not to sell your eBook on any other platform. You will not be able to list your book on Apple Books or Barnes & Noble. So, Amazon is essentially claiming exclusive rights to something they're going to give away for free. Only you, as the author, can decide whether the exposure is beneficial enough, or if you prefer to refrain from releasing your title free of charge to Kindle Unlimited subscribers. (Warning: Online businesses change their policies more than Apple sends updates to your phone. This might not be current, just be sure you read all their fine print.)

Amazon Expanded Distribution is an option for paperback publications that broadens the accessibility to your title for bookstores, online retailers, libraries, and academic institutions. These organizations often prefer to purchase their copies from large distributors rather than via the pay-per-print model on Amazon.com. Enrolling your title in expanded distribution therefore permits additional purchasing power to brick and mortar bookstores or educational institutions and libraries. Additionally, expanded distribution is only accessible to titles that are produced with certain trim sizes, paper and ink colors, and languages. More about title eligibility can be found at Amazon.

•••••

Scott: Speaking just for me, I don't see the benefit of KDP Select. There wasn't a direct increase in the sales of *The Blue Rose* magazine when we allowed people to read a selected issue for free. For a while, I let one issue of the magazine be a part of the KDP Select club so maybe a reader would read one issue for free, and then be interested in buying the rest. I never noticed an increase in sales nor an increase in profit by allowing a copy to be free.

Amazon faces its own scrutiny in the print-on-demand publishing world. Although it's one of the easiest platforms to use for those unfamiliar with how to self-publish, it's pretty much highway robbery when it comes to royalties. Additionally, brick and mortar stores don't love working with Amazon, even if your title is available for expanded distribution (Note: you may be able to get around this by ordering author copies and selling on consignment.) However, for first-time authors searching for a quick and straight-forward way to get their manuscript in-hand, Amazon KDP is a great method.

There is much to complain about Amazon as a company. I am the first to say that I think Amazon is ruining the true fabric of American small business by selling products for less than they pay to put places out of business and then raise the price after they do (Google it), and Jeff Besos may not be a perfect human being (look into his treatment of employees, profit sharing, and donations to charity.) But because of Amazon's policy that anyone can print a book, it has allowed someone with a book idea to get it out there.

The first book I ever released on my own was *Scott Luck Stories*, an eBook-only comic essay collection of my life as a stay-at-home dad and my time in corporate America. I never sold very many, and I would never have been able to release *Scott Luck Stories* if it wasn't for Amazon. As a new author, you may not have another choice but to sign up with Amazon. They will take a big cut of the money, but it isn't Amazon that is evil, it is the consumer who is evil. They don't want to go to Fayettevillemafiapress.com and buy the book directly from FMP. They want to order it from Amazon because it is easier and for some unknown reason, they feel it is safer. What they don't understand is that Amazon is taking a huge cut and that cut is coming out of the author's pocket. Americans like big companies and big-time winners. Everyone knows Amazon doesn't pay taxes, but no one cares. They offer free shipping, so take it. Consumers like helping the big guy and not the little guy. When you are starting out, you can't fight it. I never share the link to Amazon for my products, I always share the link to my personal webpage, but I know when I make an appearance on a podcast or radio show my books are going to rise up the Amazon bestseller list because that is where readers are gonna go. Your hippy friend is going to tell you how awful you are by helping Amazon. But I bet they bought their XBox on Amazon and just didn't tell you. Fight the fight somewhere else because you won't be able to fight it with your art until you are huge. And once you are, Americans will want to give you the money directly because you will have made it. I don't get it, but I don't fight it.

Chapter Takeaways

1. Consider the advantages and disadvantages of a traditional publisher v. self-publishing.

2. Decide if you want to do POD or a short print run.

3. Understand the differences between major publishing platforms like Book Baby, Amazon, and IngramSpark.

How Do I Design a Cover?

You can't judge a book by its cover, sure, but everyone else does so you might as well accept that now. A book cover serves many reasons beyond a certain element of attraction for readers aimlessly wandering around bookstores. It should be purposefully and thoughtfully designed with both the content and the consumer in mind. A good cover will communicate the story artistically, no matter how simplistic or intricate.

Additionally, a book cover is one of the first marketing tools you'll develop. As soon as you have an idea for a book, begin thinking about the cover. True, it is a fun and productive distraction from actually writing the manuscript, but it also serves as a promotional and motivational tool throughout the process. You need time to engage an audience and build anticipation for the release, so marketing your work before it's even written can be crucial to your book's success.

Most traditional publishing companies want a year to promote the book before release. In that year, they are showing the cover design to bookstores, wholesalers, and end readers. Remember that our goal for you is that you can function like a traditional publisher with the agency and empowerment of self-publishing. So, the first step in marketing your work is to get that cover done and get it out there. Even if it's not the final design, get it as close as possible and start promoting the heck out of it. When the time comes to finalize the design for publication, be careful not to change it too much so that readers still feel familiar with the title. Post it on social media (*See Chapter 6 for more information*) and Goodreads. The cover is, sadly in many ways, more important than the content of your book. It truly is that critical to your success on the entire project.

Whatever you do, don't drop your book like a Beyoncé record. One, because, try as you might, you're not Beyoncé. But secondly, you need to give yourself time to promote and collect pre-orders. Now, this process may look slightly different if you solely intend to let Amazon do the leg work and you don't intend to manage sales outside of that platform. However, especially if you plan on ordering author copies and selling on your own terms (more on that later), spending time on promotions and taking pre-orders is key to knowing how many books you should print. You can't collect pre-orders without a book cover. Amazon and other websites won't even allow you to list a book unless you have a cover. So, in many cases, this is the very first step to publishing. Whether you have a manuscript started or not, you'd better be thinking about that cover art.

•••••

Scott: While I was still working on *Moonlighting: An Oral History*, I came up with the idea of my next book. In 2022, David Lynch's film *Twin Peaks: Fire Walk With Me* would celebrate its 30th anniversary. I figured that would be a great time to do a book on that movie. I was still in the thick of *Moonlighting*. I didn't have time to even plan out what the next book would be. But I did design a cover. So in 2022, I will release *Fire Walk With Me: Your Laura Disappeared*, and, even at this time in 2021, I haven't written a word for it. But I have a cover. I knew I had to put that cover as the last page in my *Moonlighting* book to let readers know what I was doing next. (The cover is seen to the right.)

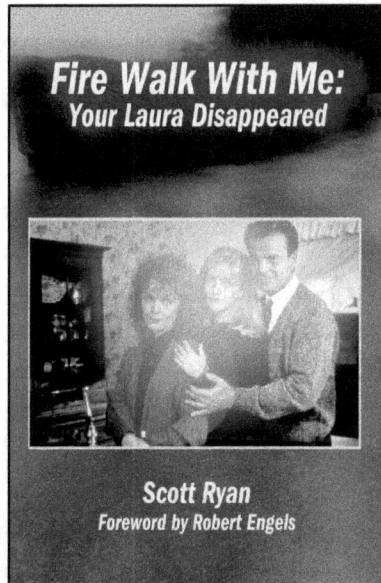

Fire Walk With Me:
Your Laura Disappeared

Scott Ryan
Foreword by Robert Engels

I designed this cover on my own. I will walk you through why I did each thing. The font is the exact font that *Fire Walk With Me* used in the opening credits. I was able to google how to recreate it, so the font will subconsciously register with fans of the film. The blurred picture that covers the entire cover is taken at the actual location where one of the famous scenes from *Twin Peaks* was filmed. (For those of you who are fans, that is a blurred picture of the giant log where Laura's body washes up.) The picture in the middle is a publicity picture—therefore allowed to be used in a critical analysis—of the main cast who play a family. I put a bright light that blurs out actress Sheryl Lee. She plays Laura Palmer in the movie. I am making her disappear which connects with my subtitle "Your Laura Disappeared," which is a crucial line from the film. I also am announcing the foreword is written by Robert Engels, who is the co-screenwriter of the film. Engels' name on the cover gives the book some gravitas and lets readers know that it is sanctioned by someone involved in the film.

Whether a reader gets all of this immediately or not, I know the cover represents the book. Now, someone else might do a different cover. Someone else might really hate what I did, (if I post it online, I guarantee you someone will tell me "it" and "I" suck within moments) but I have a reason for each item on that cover. That is good enough for me.

DIY or Don't?

If you have the tools necessary to make your cover come to life, by all means run with it. But, if you have no skill set to execute a professional and captivating cover, your best bet is to leave it to the professionals. Honestly, even if you have the skill set, you might want to leave this one to a professional. The cover is the first thing people are going to see when they find your book. Don't rely on Amazon's "look inside" feature to sell the product because that won't be there until the book is finished—entice them first with the cover art. The cover communicates with a reader in a unique way and therefore shouldn't be taken lightly.

Whether you're planning on hiring a designer (which we strongly suggest) or are more the do-it-yourself type (you better have already designed something else and have some skills in Photoshop), develop a few ideas and see them in action before making any final decisions. To get an idea of what your cover might look like, you could use a web-based application like Canva.com to insert elements of your cover and layout some potential designs. Or, if you have the software available to you, programs like Adobe Illustrator, InDesign or Photoshop can give you a platform to design your concept. Erin even suggests printing out your cover design, trimming up the edges, and taping it to a printed book to see how it feels. Visualization is key.

Considerations for Covers:

- Keep it clean and clear. No one likes a cluttered book cover and too much content will distract from the title.
- Use text purposefully and choose fonts that are easy to read.
- Keep imagery relevant and audience-appropriate.
- Do not use copyrighted images, trademarks, or logos without explicit written permission.
- If you're having difficulty finding a designer, find out who produced some of your favorite book covers and reach out to them.
- Make sure the quality of the image you use is high-res or else it will appear pixelated.

•••••

Erin: I found the cover design of my first book to be an entertaining challenge. As a designer with a background in digital marketing, I enjoyed putting together a collection of images, text, and colors to portray what the contents of the book would share with readers. I wanted the imagery to capture the attention of shoppers and intrigue someone to understand the story behind the title. Now, here's the truly bizarre occurrence that I cannot guarantee with any certainty you will experience...I spent a few weeks experimenting with a variety of designs and layouts before my final design came to me—get this—in a dream.

Gui Ren: Extraordinary Stories of Ordinary People is about the relationships I formed and the lessons I learned while navigating Southeast Asia alone. The adventures ensued after my dream job fell apart before my eyes, and I had to find a way to seize the lemonade, or make the lemons, or whatever. As I was working on the book and brainstorming covers, I had a strange dream that I was drawing a yellow circle in chalk over and over and over again. I kept tracing this yellow circle for what felt like an entire night's worth of sleep. Naturally, I woke up confused. I hate yellow, and out of all the interesting things I could have done with my dream state, I chose to draw a circle.

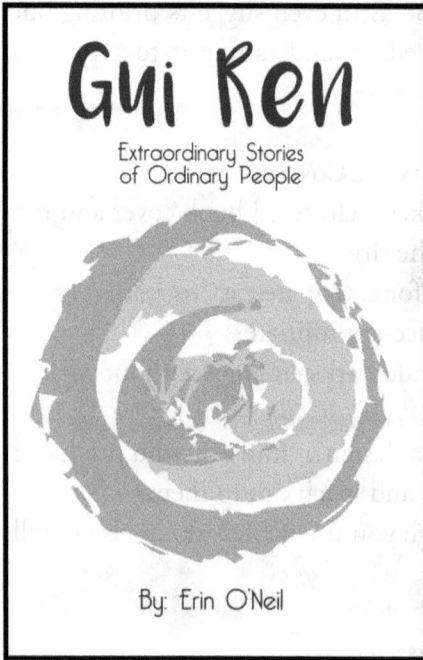

Gui Ren

Extraordinary Stories
of Ordinary People

By: Erin O'Neil

As I went throughout my day, the imagery stuck with me. That's when I realized the symbolic elements in that seemingly unimpressive dream. Chalk is representative of learning, making mistakes, and fresh starts, all three of which defined my journey through Asia. Circles are symbolic of being well-rounded, wholesome, and grounded— traits that I aspire to resonate in everything that I do. And, the only item I would ever wear that is yellow (a color I generally despise and would never walk the runway in), is a silk scarf gifted to me by my thoughtful seatmate on a train to Xi'an, China. I wrote an entire chapter about it. That yellow circle quickly became the drive behind my cover design. Sometimes, it's the simplest of thoughts that lead to the most profound imagery.

One of the reasons I'm glad I finalized my cover design prior to finishing the manuscript was so that it could serve as a daily reminder and motivator. I made a mock up of my full cover, sized it out, had it printed on legal paper, and wrapped it neatly around a copy of one of my favorite books. I then propped it up on the bookshelf for all to see. From my living room couch it looked like I had finished the entire thing. Friends and family would pick it up when they came over, confused that I had already published it, but failed to tell anyone (what a silly thought). Inside, they would instead find *The Freedom Writers Diary*. To them, it was a silly visualization tool. To me, it served as a motivational tool that pushed me to work toward my goal and turn that mock-up cover into a published book.

•••••

Scott: You probably won't be surprised by this, but I actually don't know everything. Yeah, it is obvious to you, but it came as quite a shock to me. I had been designing CD covers for my cousin Lisa since 1997. I was also a wiz at creating comic memes. So, when it came time to design my cover for *The Last Days Of Letterman*, I knew I was the person to do it. Here is the cover I designed:

The top part of the cover was from a picture I took in New York City of Letterman's marquee. The bottom picture was of Dave running across the stage during the last episode on *The Late Show*. I loved it because it summed up my book. You wouldn't get a direct view of David Letterman, but rather a passing view of him as told from the writers and producers who had worked with him for thirty years. Genius, right? Well, guess what? Everyone hated it. I mean everyone. The feedback I got was something like: "It is too wordy." "The color of the yellow in the title doesn't match the yellow in the picture of the marquee." "It's too busy." "You can't tell that is Letterman running." If you weren't a diehard fan, you probably wouldn't even know Dave ran across the stage before every episode. A book has to appeal to a mass audience if you want to make any money. Yes, you want to stay true to your vision, but compromise is good. (Sondheim says, "A vision's just a vision if it's only in your head. If no one gets to hear it, it's as good as dead." "Putting it Together," *Sunday in the Park With George*, 1985.)

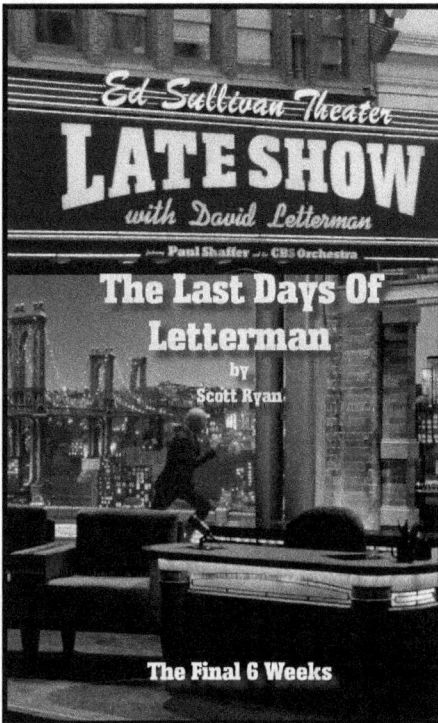

When our distributor pitched the book to the Barnes & Noble, they said they liked the Letterman concept, but they would never carry that book in their store. The cover was horrible and the inside was an absolute mess. (Did I mention that I designed the inside of the book as well?) Our distributor told me I had to hire a designer to do both if I wanted anyone to carry the book. They had a person in mind. His name was Mark Karis. For $1,500 he would design the cover. For another $1,500 he would design the inside of the book. (Did I mention that all this happened two months before we had to go to print to make our pub date?)

So, I hired Mark Karis, for $3,000 and he designed this cover:

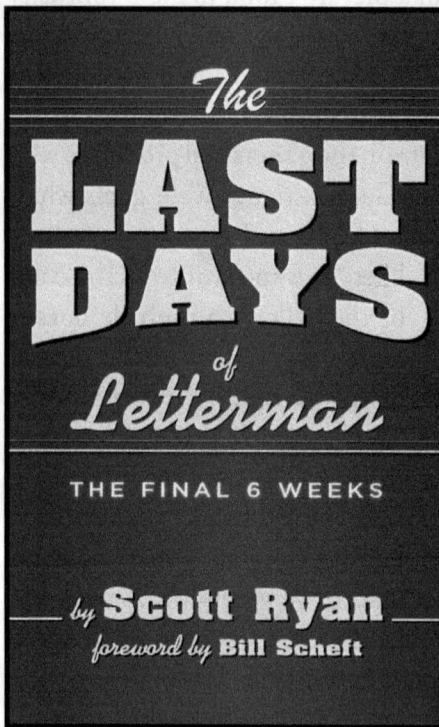

Surprise, surprise. I hated it. I remember when I first opened the email, I really wanted to cry. It had no personal connection to Letterman. Watching Letterman every day from 1986-2015, was the longest relationship I had with anyone in my life. This cover took away my personal connection. It was just, blah. It was all text. The photo of Dave running was important to me. I was crushed. Well, here comes another non-surprise: Everyone loved it. The distributor flipped for it. My business partner loved it. Barnes & Noble carried it and many stores picked it for their display models. As of this printing, *The Last Days of Letterman* is FMP's biggest seller. (Not the most profitable book, but that is another can of worms.)

So, how could that be? How could I have been so wrong? Or was I? Here is what I learned from the experience and what I hope you can learn from it. The reason Mark's cover was better was because it was clean, concise, and easy to digest. The font and color made viewers associate with Letterman without using any copyrighted material. With more space available on the front cover, he was able to add the fact that the foreword of the book was written by one of Dave's comedy writers, Bill Scheft. Where would that have fit on my version? The running picture meant something to me, but that was it. We ultimately compromised by using the photo on the back cover. I can't say I love the cover, but I realized I had a lot to learn about cover design before I attempted another. Learning and growing is key to being a success in any industry. Not sure if I've learned enough yet because you will notice that Erin did the cover of this book. So there's that.

•••••

Whether you choose to tackle the task on your own, or hire a designer, give yourself time to brainstorm and process the many versions that arise. Challenge yourself to consider not just how you envision the book, but what consumers respond best to. Simplify your concept and then simplify it twice more before running it by a third party. Develop a few versions and test it with friends and family. Do some research to see how other book covers of similar genres were designed. If you notice, the cover to this book is an actual picture we took. We did that because every book about this topic used some sort of computer graphic, so we wanted to use an actual photo to stand out. Maybe we succeeded and that is why you bought the book. Scroll through Amazon and note which elements you love and don't love about other works. This may just help you develop a keener eye for concise and professional book design.

If you decide to work with a designer, be as specific with your vision as possible. Or, if you're not quite sure where to go with your concept, consult with them and allow them to bring their creativity to the table. You might just be pleasantly surprised with what they produce. No matter what, be flexible and appreciate that you are pursuing a professional's input for a reason, particularly if they can backup their designs with proven strategies for marketing and sales. Trust them. If you're not sure where to find a designer, you could start by searching for contractors on websites like Upwork, Freelancer, or Fiverr. (Pssssst...Scott and Erin also do this for a living.)

Back Cover/Spine

Your back cover doesn't need to be designed until you are ready to go to print. So, don't feel like you have to skip ahead to this task just yet. This is also true of the spine. In fact, you can't confidently design the full cover or spine because you won't know the dimensions until your PDF is created and the page count is finalized. This means you will have to write and design the entire book before you can move on to the final steps of cover design. Drafting out imagery is always a great idea! Just don't go sizing anything until the manuscript is complete. Only then will the printer, whether it is print on demand or a short run, provide the dimensions for your full cover. It will look something like this:

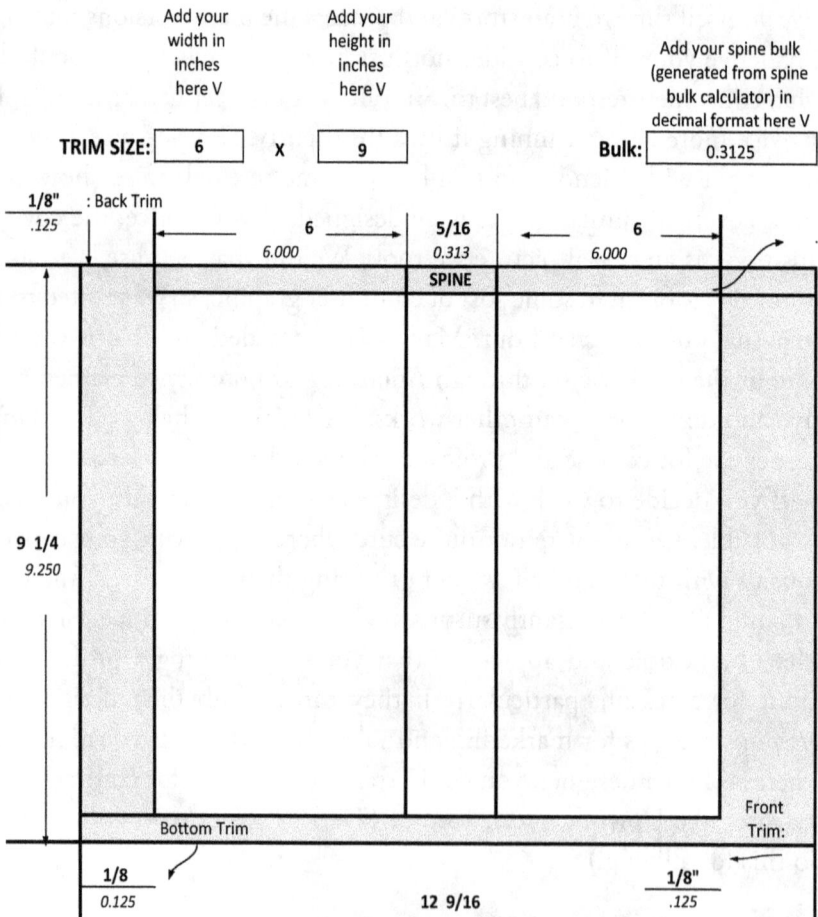

	Add your width in inches here V		Add your height in inches here V			Add your spine bulk (generated from spine bulk calculator) in decimal format here V
TRIM SIZE:	6	X	9		Bulk:	0.3125

1/8" : Back Trim
.125

6	5/16	6
6.000	0.313	6.000

SPINE

9 1/4
9.250

Bottom Trim

Front Trim:

1/8	12 9/16	1/8"
0.125		.125

The easiest way to build this is by using Adobe Illustrator, which allows you to create a file sized to the exact measurements. On the previous image, which was for FMP's *A Diva is a Version of a Female Wrestler* by Scarlett Harris, I created a file that was 12.813 inches across and 9.25 inches top to bottom. Now, if this scares you because you have no idea what I am talking about, you may want to hire someone to design your cover. If you miscalculate by a fraction of an inch, the spine of your book is going to print off-center and you won't be happy. We promise.

For your back cover you will want to include your author photo, a website where people can order your books, a description of the book, your publisher's logo, a barcode with the price and ISBN number (see Chapter 9), and maybe a photo of Letterman running across the stage. (Some grudges last forever.) It is always preferable if you match the color scheme of the front cover. The cover, spine, and backcover should all complement each other and be created from the same palette. (See Chapter 7 for more on this.)

Chapter Takeaways

1. Start on your cover design early, because you should be using it as a marketing tool before you even finish writing the book.

2. Consider getting a professional to design your cover.

3. You will have to design a spine and back cover later on.

CHAPTER SIX

How Do I Promote My Book?

There is excitement in the anticipation of something. Think about your favorite movie trailer that comes out a year before the release or the season cliffhanger for your favorite show that won't return until the fall. You might hate the wait, but the wait creates excitement. In the end, finally getting that new season or brand new movie in your hands is that much more rewarding. It's complicated—we know. But what really drives people is the wait and anticipation. So, as soon as possible, get your cover design out into the world. The cover image should be your profile picture on Facebook, Twitter, Instagram, and everywhere else you exist on the internet. Your audiences will learn to associate your name with your book, and the time you spend interacting with others online can be all the more impactful. The goal is to let your book steep in the minds of readers; introduce a new flavor, let it steep, and JUST before it cools off, give them what they really want: the full flavor. Serve it too hot or too cold and you'll either scare people away or lose their interest entirely. We're aiming for Goldilocks here, people. Give your social media a chance to turn likes and shares into dollars and cents. Give your cover design an opportunity to generate the interest you need to drive the most sales.

We strongly suggest you get on every social media platform there is. This will provide further opportunity for you to reach unique audiences with a variety of interests and communication preferences. You never know when a retweet will put your book in front of someone who might want to order your book in bulk. (The writer's dream, am I right?)

Let's say the name of your book is *A Deer at the Feeder*. Whether it's a work of fiction, personal narrative, sci-fi, or young adult, you are going to want to get that idea out everywhere. While you are busy writing about that cute little deer and the feeder, you want people to see that cover as they're indulging in their daily scrolling binge. Post regularly but not so frequently that people search for the 'unfollow' button. The best strategy is to post once a day or once every other day with content about your idea, book, or relevant recent events and articles. Simply posting your cover every day will not be as effective as mixing it in with similar content. Get creative. Incorporate other aspects of your idea. Engage audiences with the content without giving away the full manuscript.

Follow other accounts who post about deer and engage intentionally with them. Find articles about feeders and post them. Always include a link to your book. If you are selling your book on your own website, share that link. Even if you are publishing on Amazon, prioritize marketing your website or other pre-ordering platform. We never send people to Amazon. Trust us, Amazon is doing just fine. We want you to direct customers to your website to help build a brand and encourage future engagement. Do you have a newsletter? Now is the time to capture interest and gain a wider audience. Your book can be a tool to inform readers of your other products and services. So, again, if given the chance, post your book to your website or social media outlet, and direct people there before defaulting to Amazon. If you don't have a website, then send them to Amazon.

Social media can be nauseating, yes, but it can also be your key to building an audience, engaging with followers, and ramping up anticipation for the publication day. Even if social networking just isn't your thing, you can use it to harness the power of widespread communication and promotion to better sell your work. We're not telling you to share what you ate for breakfast. No one cares. We're telling you that without social media, your marketing efforts will be a waste. The strategy to promote your self-published book doesn't have to be as complex as one might think. In fact, it can be as simple as posting behind the scenes photos of your writing setup at a coffee shop or interviewing a subject for your manuscript. The point is to continuously engage viewers with relevant content to remind them that a book is coming and that they should be excited about it.

If you already use social media, you'll need to decide how much you want to blend your existing accounts with your new promotional material. If you intend to blend personal with business and share publicity posts on your existing page, you may not need to set up separate accounts or additional pages. Some authors like to keep their private life private. Others want to open their doors to their readers to show them how they are just the same. But, if you are going to share the doodles your child colored at school and then follow that up with the cover of your upcoming book, you may want to rethink having just one platform. We can't give you advice on what you want to share with the world. However, keep in mind that as your audience grows you may want to separate the two. Once you've established a following, you won't want to tell everyone they need to go follow the new page. You will lose some readers, guaranteed (because grandma inevitably won't be able to find your new page). So, take the following advice into consideration while maintaining awareness of what's going to work best for your book and your personal privacy.

facebook

Erin: Facebook is a great place for photos, vlogs, blog posts, polls, live videos, and more. It's an easy way to reach a lot of people and manage followers on a platform you're likely already familiar with. If you're erring on the side of attracting a larger audience, set up a Facebook page (not a group) specifically dedicated to your book and/or your publishing company. Take the time to properly set up the page before inviting Aunt Sue and Uncle Jimmy to hit the follow button. This means adding a profile picture, cover photo, page description, about section (shorter than the full description), email, and, if you have it, a website. You'll want people to say, "Wow, this is legit!" when they investigate your invitation. If it's anything close to, "What in the spam have I been notified about?" your page will melt back into the never-ending pits of the internet.

•••••

Scott: Should you desire, you can purchase Facebook ads that can be directed to people who are not following you but who have expressed interest in the topic you are writing about. If we are using *A Deer at the Feeder* as an example, we could target an ad directly to people who say they like deer, nature, or even hunting (who knows, maybe there's a hunter out there with a soft spot). Facebook ads will help attract people who are outside of your inner circle.

Instagram

Erin: Otherwise referred to by Scott as "Instapuke," Instagram is a primarily image-based mobile application. Use this platform to share photos, short videos, or go live to further interact with followers. This is a great way to run giveaways, interact with similar accounts, balance behind-the-scenes sneak peeks with classic promotions, and visually engage readers by inviting them into your work. The only downside to Instagram is that links in a post cannot be clicked. So, set your bio website to wherever you want to direct people for your book and be sure to let them know to peep your bio for the link.

Protip: because you can only put one link in your bio, you might want to create a Linktree. It's a free way to offer followers multiple URL destinations through just one primary link. If you have a website, YouTube channel, and blog, for example, you can easily link all three. You can even personalize the colors and style of your Linktree! When you post about your book on Instagram, you can add #linkinbio to let people know how to find your website. Also, keep in mind that any posts you share to Instagram can be automatically forwarded to your Facebook page if you choose to connect the accounts. Although, strangely enough, it doesn't go the other way around unless you use the creator studio page of your business Facebook account. Use this feature to make the most of your time and content when it comes to cross-promotional material.

•••••

Scott: I just want to point out that the main reason I call it "Instapuke" is because this platform is the ultimate example of the 1% in America. It annoys me beyond belief that Instagram only allows people who have 10,000 followers or more to put links to their products on their post. This means if you are already struggling to point people to your website because you have a small following, Instagram makes it even harder. Social media should level the playing field and not allow the *haves* to dominate the *have nots*. If I could put Instapuke in the guillotine and say, "Off with its head," I would. That being said, I use it, but I have no idea if it drives sales because I can't put a link up. My guess is it drives sales of my books to Amazon and not me. "Off with its head," I say again.

The key to instagram is to have engaging content and to use hashtags to your advantage. The more hashtags you use, the greater chance your post might be discovered. A great protip is to have a document on your phone that has all the hashtags you use. That way, when you do a post, you can just copy that list in the bottom of your post instead of typing the hashtags out every time. So, if I am doing a *Blue Rose* magazine post, I can open up the document that has all the *Twin Peaks* hashtags and just copy it right in. This saves time and creates consistency. Example: #TwinPeaks #DavidLynch #BlueRoseMagazine #SherylLee #lauraPalmer #MarkFrost #AgentCooper #FWWM. There is nothing fun about typing those same hashtags every time you post on your phone. Do it once and then you are done. This also is a great idea for Twitter posts.

twitter

Scott: Twitter is your best friend if your goal is reaching people you don't know. I have had several authors tell me they don't like twitter, but I can tell you I have had 75% of my success come from twitter. Twitter allows you to connect with anyone and everyone for free. The key to Twitter is the hashtag. When I am promoting *The Blue Rose*, all my tweets have #TwinPeaks #DavidLynch #LauraPalmer. When I am talking about my *Moonlighting* book, #Moonlighting #BruceWillis #CybillShepherd. For promoting this book, it's been a steady diet of #selfpublishing #authors #newbooks. The trick is, you need to know who is interested in what you are writing. If you don't know who wants your book, how do you expect anyone else to help sell it?

You also want to follow people who you think will be interested. So, follow local bookstores and retweet their stuff. For our *Deer* book, follow those hashtags and be sure to like and support other people in your genre. If you are writing mystery books, then follow mystery Twitter accounts, or people who post about Agatha Christie or whatever author you like. You need to find your people and get in with them. You will not make it alone in the social media world and no one will help you learn it. (That isn't actually true. No one will help you learn it for free. There are plenty of people you can pay to do it, but you are basically paying them to do what we just told you to do. Follow. Retweet. Like.)

When I can't sleep, I pull up Twitter and search for #thirtysomething or #moonlighting and then like every tweet that refers to the TV show from my account about that book. My hope is that person will see that like and say, "There is a book about *thirtysomething*? This is the best day of my life, and I am gonna buy that book." Does it happen often? No. But I was just lying there listening to my wife snore as she dreams that one of my books will take off and then she will love me for real.

Do you need a twitter account for each of your books? I think you do. Is that a pain? You bet it is. Working social media will probably take up the exact same time as writing does. That is a horrible reality, but it is a fact. On the days that I don't tweet, I don't sell. If you are writing a teenage vampire saga, then you could get away with having one twitter account called @bitesNZits. You could also use this account to promote each book in your trilogy. But, if you have one book about vampires getting their first monthly and your next book is about the corporation of the United States Senate, get two different twitter accounts and two different Facebook pages and maybe some counseling because you probably need it. It also works best if you can get the same handle (name) on Twitter and Instagram, use the same icon photo for all platforms, and schedule them so every post goes to each platform*. (*Protip from **Erin:** use a program like Hootsuite or Later to schedule all of your content in advance and post across all platforms at one time. Rather than making three separate posts for Facebook, Instagram, and Twitter, just make one and have Hootsuite do the rest. Easy peasy! You are your own publicist.)

TikTok

Erin: Honestly, TikTok is a continuously evolving entity that has fallen under quite a bit of scrutiny in the United States. Regardless, TikTok is simply another place to connect with audience members and share your work. It's a platform to display your creativity, tell your story, and put out entertaining content that will hopefully drive people to your website and/or other accounts.

In the case of the *Deer*, you might start a TikTok profile that is built around sharing fun facts about deer. Your content may not be specific to what your book is actually about, but think of this as a method to connect interests. It's kind of like the *inspired by your purchases* section of your Amazon home page. If your followers enjoy deer facts, there is a chance they may also enjoy reading a book entitled *A Deer at the Feeder*. Your goal is to guide your audience and help them realize that if they enjoy your social media content, they will also probably enjoy your written work.

• • • • •

Scott: I don't know what a TikTok is.

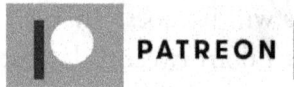

PATREON

Erin: What if I told you that you could share your behind the scenes content and *get paid to do it*? Patreon offers creatives a way to offer exclusive access to certain content for different tiers of paying subscribers. It's like Facebook, but monetized, in *your* favor. Who knew?! For $5 a month, subscribers might get a monthly update from you about how the manuscript is progressing. For $10, they'd get the previous tier plus sneak peeks of the chapters. For $20 a month they'd get all of the above, plus a discount on the future publication and a signed bookmark. For $50 they'd get the whole darn deal and then maybe receive a free signed copy as well as a listing of their name on your social media as a primary supporter. The possibilities are endless!

You, as the creator, can get creative with the rewards and the content you share. This is not only a great way to engage audience members with behind the scenes content, but also to reward investors with exclusive looks into your writing process and the finished work. Patreon is a fantastic way to boost funding for your project and have additional money to put into marketing to the general public. Patreon was responsible for sourcing much of the start-up costs for my business and allowed me to set aside paid work in the interest of finishing the book and getting it out to the masses. Without it, I'm not sure I could have spent the intentional time that I did writing and strategizing for a successful launch. In addition to finishing *Gui Ren*, Patreon enabled me to donate time to student groups and various storytelling initiatives to further my profession and develop my skills.

•••••

Scott: I am just not a fan of GoFundMe or Patreon. It doesn't mean they are bad. Many people have had a load of success with them. It just doesn't sit well with me. I think it is because for so many years I created movies and CDs on my own. I never asked anyone to help pay for them. I create art for myself because I have to do it to live. I do offer preorders for my books and in many ways that is a form of this, but I like that my reader actually gets that book in the end. I think this is just a generational thing. I am from Gen X, and it is hard for my generation to ask for something outright because we were raised to be seen and not heard.

🐵 mailchimp

Scott: Mailchimp is an email service that allows you to send out mass emails. If your email database is under 2,000, the service is free. This saves you from having to email the link for your new book to each one of the people who ordered your last book. This has been a pretty helpful tool for *Blue Rose* subscribers. Every time a new subscription package opens up, I can let them know pretty easily. Mailchimp has a really easy set up that allows you to upload photos of your product, link them directly to your website, and write a nice email. The major disadvantage is that if the person has a Gmail account, which is honestly most people, the email might automatically be filtered to the promotional web tab and is therefore probably never seen by the subscriber. You can ask people to mark your email address as not junk mail, but how many of them really will?

They have a lot of nice statistics for you to look at, but it usually just breaks my heart. Here are the figures for my latest email from *The Blue Rose*:

25% off (copy 05)	Sent	**44.3%**	**2.2%**
Regular · Scott Ryan Productions		Opens	Clicks
Sent Mon, January 4th 9:55 AM to 1K			
recipients by you			

This email didn't go to just random people. It went to customers who had purchased thirteen of the fifteen issues that we published. That means they really are interested in getting the information that there is a new package to get issues 14 & 15. Even with that discounted package, only 44% of the emails were opened and only 2% clicked the link in it. I am sure they want to know there is a new issue, but most likely Gmail filtered the email out and the person never saw it. Looking at my sales on January 4th, I sold 12 subscriptions, which is a big day for me. I have to order 1,250 copies of the magazine, and I only sold about 700 copies of issue 15. I have to sell more than that to break even on the printing costs. So while it was a low percentage of clicks—2% of 1,000 emails is 20 people clicking and 12 purchases—that is a high percentage. Mailchimp helped keep *The Blue Rose* afloat through Covid-19 even with its limitations.

One more thing to remember. If you send all your customers to Amazon, they get to keep the email addresses of your readers, not you. The only reason I can use Mailchimp at all is because I have the emails from people who bought something from my website. This is why, even if you are printing the book from Amazon, it is better to sell it from your own website and fulfill the order yourself. You will make more money because Amazon won't take a cut of the sale, and you will get the contact information from someone who is actually interested in your work. However, you will also have to ship the product yourself, which has never been a downside to me because I love getting to see Shameeka at the post office. Also, remember not to annoy your customers with an email every day or even every week. I only send an email out for major announcements. I also keep track of when they buy, and I remove them from that list so no one gets an email for something they already bought. You wouldn't believe the amount of complex spreadsheets I have that keep track of each purchase. I do this because I do not want anyone to block my emails.

A Social Media Warning

Scott: Just about everyone is on social media, so you know the dangers without us getting too deep into them. But, if this is your first time putting out a product through social media, you should be prepared for something: HATE. Before I started *The Blue Rose*, I was posting on my personal Facebook page all the time. I posted funny, crazy statements. I shot my mouth off about politics. I posted pictures of my food. I was just like everyone else. After I saw that I could sell my product by posting on the above-mentioned platforms, I started to mix my comic posts in with my business posts. All of my posts before were understood because my connections were with all my friends, and they knew I was just a comic at heart. Once my platforms were opened to strangers (AKA readers), things changed.

Suddenly, my jokes about hating my kids, my self-deprecating comments about my art, or my political rants were taken as gospel. People either took me directly at my word (because there is no such thing as satire on the internet) or even worse, they came back with hate. Over the years, I have been mocked for my art, accused of lies, and my work has been criticized in the most debased and lowest form. I have been attacked personally, received hate emails, even been reported, blocked, and temporarily banned from platforms. The final laugh was on them: I do not find my self worth from feedback from others. (I have no self worth, so they can't affect it.) But this warning is for you, especially if you take internet comments to heart or even worse equate them with professional feedback. If you are going to step out into the sun and try to share your work, the world's reaction will ALWAYS be to try to make you step back into the shade. Any one who tries to do something will *always* be attacked. Know yourself. Know your worth. Ignore the hate.

•••••

Erin: It's easy to get sucked into the fads. I mean, trends are catchier than "It's a Small World." They're not just intended to capture your attention, the goal is to keep you entertained and attentive…forever. TikTok is perhaps the worst culprit of them all. Continuous scrolling is a dangerous path to venture down, and social media can quickly become a bigger time suck than intended. This is why using something like Hootsuite, where you don't even have to visit your profiles in order to post content, can be helpful in maintaining a balance. Should you respond to your followers and interact with other accounts? Yes. Should you make an attempt at cross-promotions and giveaways? Sure. But should you spend hours on social media a day to market one book? No. At that point, you may be in too deep. Social media pits are deep. Stay aware of your usage and don't let your promotional efforts take away valuable time from actually finishing the manuscript.

Remind Me Again, Why Should I Promote Early?

If you promote your book and no one orders it or engages purposefully with your accounts over time, that might let you know just how interested people are in your topic. This will also help you track what is working. If you have a successful post on Facebook and the next day your pre-orders are up, do that again. Everything you do is collecting data. That is the best way to look at it. So, if one of your posts receives no likes or does not influence preorders, it wasn't a waste of time. It was you figuring out what works best.

Additionally, if you are selling copies from your website or in-person at events, the more pre-orders your book gets in those months before release, the more data you will have to make the decision of how many copies you are going to need to print. This is both a logistics strategy and an opportunity to increase capital so that when the time comes to order your copies, you're not blindly investing in a book that hasn't had the time to circulate. Generating interest before the book is done will help you understand your audience and more effectively approach sales when you're ready to launch.

Chapter Takeaways

1. Promote early and often. In fact, do it right now on every platform you can.

2. Don't just focus on the contents of your book, mix up your posts by sharing other articles, recent events, trends, or even memes that are relevant to your title.

3. Do not waste time looking at social media, and never respond to hateful comments.

CHAPTER SEVEN

Which Software Should I Use?

Although this seems like a chapter that should come earlier in the process, if you've learned anything by now, we hope it's that promotions and reader engagement should be the first steps after solidifying your book idea. The writing is important—you can't have a book without it—but what good is writing if no one knows it exists?

You have your cover, your book is circulating the internet, and now you need to write the thing. The days in which you might grab a yellow legal pad and a pencil and sit down to write are long gone. The typewriter is a thing of the past. For good reason, too, considering a single hard copy of your manuscript is more likely to catch fire, according to Murphy's Law. You will want backups of your backups of your work, so get on your computer and start typing. If you don't have a computer, find a library and keep several jump drives on hand. You don't want to lose your work, trust us. You can write your book in Word, Google Docs, Notepad or any word processing program you would like, but it should be done digitally. When you submit the book it will need to be in a digital format. We can't imagine in 2021 that any more time needs to be spent convincing you.

•••••

Scott: The benefit of Google Docs is that your file is stored in the cloud. The beauty of this is that no matter where you are, so is your book. You won't have the excuse of, "Damn, I would work on my book, but I don't have access to it." If you say, "I don't know what the cloud is," that is OK, you don't need to understand how something works to use it. The benefit of Google Docs is that it is never going to crash. When I was getting close to going to print on a book, my wife asked if I had backed it up. I said, "If Google goes down, I think we have bigger problems in the world than me losing my book." I have worked on my book in the middle of the night on my phone, on an airplane with my laptop, and at my desk on my iMac. The book is everywhere that I am.

For this book, Erin and I wrote in the same Google Doc at the same time. That is another great feature of a Google Doc; it makes collaborating with another writer even easier. We could edit each other's sentences and *even distract each other by writing random words that make no sense like snickies*. Hey, Erin, get out of here, I am working! *I need a cookie – Love, Erin*. Oh boy, maybe Google Docs isn't for everyone, but it does have advantages because *Erin is pretty*. Dammit. She did it again.

Now that I distracted Erin with a cookie, I can tell you the other benefits. The editing feature in Google Docs is very helpful when it comes to working with your editor. You can leave notes for specific people and even assign sections for review. As the managing editor of a magazine, we have several writers working on articles over the two months when we create an issue. The writer would write their first draft and then share the document with me. I would read it and give them notes. Then our copy editor would jump in and correct the grammar and give more notes. The author would be able to fix those and see the changes. No printing and wasting paper, and no fear of losing what you did because Google Docs allows you to see the changes.

•••••

Erin: I used Ulysses to write my first book. Unlike Microsoft Word and Google Docs, Ulysses allowed me to more easily organize chapters with click-and-drag functionality and limit my workspace to one section at a time. Occasionally, I can find myself overwhelmed by the unlimited white space and hoards of ideas, each craving to be written simultaneously. With Ulysses, I found it easier to navigate the chapter titles, jot down my thoughts so they would not be forgotten, then return to my work space, free from distraction of other sections.

Ulysses is a desktop and mobile app that stores and syncs data using iCloud. It features a clean, distraction-free interface with customizable color palettes and multiple writing modes. Once users become familiar with the simple markup shortcuts, they can easily create headlines, denote important passages, insert quotes, and add comments to the text. Additionally, Ulysses makes it easy to navigate through your manuscript with keyboard shortcuts and clear hierarchical groups. One of my favorite features was the writing goal function. This enabled me to set daily, weekly, and monthly goals to encourage and track progress. If you're working within a particular timeframe or toward a specific deadline, this can help you stay on track. Its live preview function enables you to easily evaluate your work output and then easily exports into a variety of files necessary for self-publishing. Plus, if you're writing on Medium or WordPress, Ulysses works to schedule or publish directly to those platforms.

Unfortunately, Ulysses is currently only available for macOS and iOS users. It does come with a free trial so you can evaluate whether the platform will be effective for you as a writer. Additionally, there are student discounts with any valid student ID. While the monthly or annual rates are an intentional investment, I sincerely believe it is worth it. It expedited my writing process and kept my working space clean. Ulysses made it easy for me to write on the go as creativity struck because my manuscript was readily available on my laptop, desktop, and phone.

I have also used Scrivener, but that was primarily for the formatting of my eBook. Scrivener is a similar platform to Ulysses, but presents a little less modern feel. However, this application is accessible to iOS, macOS, and Windows users. Unlike Ulysses, it is a one-time purchase and offers a bundle in case you need it to sync across multiple operating systems. Scrivener is arguably the easiest way to produce an eBook—I think Scott would say the same—although, I can't say I genuinely gave Ulysses a try when it came to this particular project.

•••••

No matter which writing software you select, set goals for your word count, be intentional with your organization, and save, save, save. Whether it's a children's book that is ten pages long, or a 450-page autobiographical work, you will be devastated if one day your computer decides to rage quit or your cat dumps coffee all over your keyboard. Erin will proudly tell you that she now compulsively hits Command S on her keyboard as she's thinking about her next sentence. Auto save is great, but compulsive back ups are even greater. Wherever you store your work, make sure there's an accessible place to keep an extra copy. If the cloud is too creepy for you, grab some thumb drives. Even then, we strongly recommend an additional external hard drive. Losing your work is a writer's worst nightmare. Do what you can to prevent any major losses. Much to Bob Ross's chagrin, there are no happy accidents when your manuscript goes missing.

Additional Software

You will need a handful of other software to finish your published work. Some are affordable but difficult to use, others are an investment but will serve you greatly with efficiency and a lack of wanting to punch your fist through a wall. While IngramSpark offers a book-building tool for both interior formatting and cover design, and Amazon provides free Microsoft Word templates, these services may not always meet your needs. If you feel that your manuscript just needs standard, basic formatting, you may select your publishing platform based on the free services available to get the job done. However, if you intend to add images or customize many of the interior elements, those free services may limit your ability to do so.

Scott and Erin survive on Adobe products. Illustrator, Photoshop, and InDesign are their go-to software when it comes to cover design and interior manuscript formatting. Each has a slightly different purpose but function together to create a streamlined publishing process and establish a template for future books. That's right, after one book is done, you have a customizable, personalized template ready to accommodate your next title. Just import the manuscript over your original text, and start tweaking as necessary. Easy peasy!

The price of purchasing a year's rights to the Adobe Creative Suite can be pricey. As of the printing of this book it runs right around $670 a year, but you get access to all of their products. Neither of us could ever imagine designing a book without InDesign. When you purchase the complete package you get two email logins. We split the cost and that makes it a little easier. This is what has kept our friendship together. Erin has wanted to drop Scott for months now, but she can't because she will lose her discounted Adobe access. So the benefits are endless.

●●●●●

Erin: I actually formatted *Gui Ren* in Pages, a word processor app for iOS. It was clunky and I fudged my way around certain technical issues, but it did the trick. Fortunately, I wasn't adding in images (much to my mother's dismay) and the chapter headings were nothing complex, but I often wonder how much nicer the final book would have looked had I used a software with a little more accessibility. I ran into issues with page numbers and spent far too long managing section breaks, but I got the job done. That being said, I wouldn't recommend using Pages or Microsoft Word. You will be limited in functionality and may find it challenging to visualize the full interior design. That is where a program like Adobe InDesign or even Scrivener (in some capacities) could be more useful.

Creating a book with InDesign

Once your manuscript has been finished and you have completed all the revisions from your editor, then you need to design your book. Notice that we mentioned, "*You have completed all the revisions from your editor.*" If you're going to start formatting, the first step is to have a finished manuscript. Dumping your text into a workable file and beginning to adjust will be pointless if you still have major edits to make. Even a single word change can alter the layout. So, to prevent death threats toward your computer, do yourself a favor and finalize your text before even thinking about developing the interior book design.

InDesign provides a comprehensive software for designing and managing an interior book design. As an industry-leading tool for print and digital publication layout, InDesign supports everything from brochures, posters, reports, magazines, stationary, and books. Wrapping text around an object that is anything other than square, for example, may be difficult to do in Microsoft Word, but with InDesign there is a seamless way to make your image stand out without losing the fluidity of your text. While there can be a slight learning curve when first approaching Adobe software, the benefit of accessibility far outweighs the time spent understanding its functions.

There are several helpful features of InDesign for book formatting, including:

- Drag-and-drop page reordering
- Grid lines and ruler guides
- Text flow to help your content seamlessly carry over to the next page, regardless of the page's formatting
- Master pages for specific template needs (chapter title, section break, blank page, etc.)

This last feature is arguably the best reason to invest in InDesign. Master pages are intended to make it easier for you to design the layout by providing presets. For example, many professionally designed books have the author's name and the title of the book (or sometimes section) at the top of the pages. These are often consistent throughout the book with the author on the left and the title on the right. However, these headings are not typically seen on chapter title pages.

So, you might have at least three master page templates set up:

1. Master page with author name and page number
2. Master page with book (or section) title and page number
3. Master page with just the page number

When you need to replace a master page with a different template based on your layout, you simply drag and drop the preferred master to the page you're working on. Rather than having to fight Microsoft Word on when to apply a page number or header, InDesign does the heavy lifting for you.

InDesign offers easy access to adding photos and artwork to your project. There is a caption function that easily adds the space to add a great caption to your photo. It just helps make your PDF have that professional look to it. There are a million bells and whistles throughout the program that can overwhelm a first-time user, but don't worry about the parts that you aren't going to use, just focus on the parts you are going to use.

Designing your cover on Illustrator

In addition to interior layout, you will need to consider the specifications for designing your cover art so that it is accepted by the publishing platform. You should already have your front cover designed and it should have been circulating the internet for a while now. You may have used Adobe Illustrator, Adobe Photoshop, or a free platform like Canva.com. But, now you'll need to finish the full cover (front, back, and spine) in order to complete the exterior design.

Before diving into cover design, check in with the platform you've selected to see if they have downloadable templates or specified dimensions to use in setting up your file. They should request the trim size and a final number of pages in order to provide an accurate template. Yes, you are correct, this means the full cover design should come after you have at least formatted enough of the interior to know an approximate number of pages. If you're off by 2, it won't ruin your cover, but if you're off by 20 pages, you may have to redesign and resubmit a few things. Trust us, there's nothing worse than getting to the time of submission and realizing you left 0.25" off of the file size. It's a minuscule amount, but will be all the more aggravating for that exact reason.

Adobe Illustrator makes it easy for you to set up a template, layer images and text, and adjust your file to meet the needs of your publishing platform. Ruler guides can be helpful when setting margins and aligning objects within your design. Plus, if you have an Adobe package that includes Illustrator and Photoshop, any updates you make to an image via Photoshop will automatically sync with your cover design in Illustrator; no need to reimport the file.

Creating an eBook

If you are only doing an eBook, then there isn't as much design to be done. One of the things that is great about eBooks is the reader decides the design. When you are designing a hard copy, the designer picks the font size, picture placement and the amount of words that are on a page. In an eBook, the reader picks those things on their eBook reader device, be it Kindle, Apple Books, or Nook. That frees the designer to not have to worry too much about the overall design of the eBook. Unlike print, where your interior design can greatly impact a reader's experience, eBooks are quite limited in terms of layout. Outside of on-the-go reading, the primary benefit and bonus functionality to eBooks is, instead of referencing a website or link in your text, you can actually link it.

•••••

Scott: Amazon and Apple Books both have programs that allow you to create an eBook or an iBook on their platform. I use a different program. It is called Scrivener. It only costs $49 and if you are going to write more than one book, you will certainly get your money's worth out of it. It allows you to create PDFs, Epubs and Kindle versions simultaneously. You can purchase a license at www.literatureandlatte.com/scrivener.

I have created every issue of *The Blue Rose* and every eBook FMP has published using Scrivener, and I have never had an issue. I like having the control to design the eBook as I see fit, instead of leaving it up to someone else. A side benefit that I can't really explain is the spell check in Scrivener seems to be better than Google Docs or InDesign. I always run the spell check on each program and they all seem to catch different ones. The last thing I create is the eBook, and I always find at least one spelling error through Scrivener. Now, it is true, I might just be a bad speller. (I really, really am.) But I think having different programs run a check is a great tip. The other really nice thing that Scrivener does is it automatically keeps the footnotes, italics and special characters when you copy them from InDesign to Scrivener. This saves you a ton of work. This does not happen when you copy from Google Doc or Word to InDesign.

A negative for Scrivener is that I have had trouble getting indents to work sometimes, but I have always been able to work around that. I have actually gotten around the chapter title issue by just capturing my titles as a photo. That way I can display the font and it looks exactly as it looks in my hardcopy design. What I mean by this is instead of typing out "Chapter 1 His Girl Maddie" and then fighting with the Kindle or eBook rules to get it centered or colored the way I want it, I just load this as a photo that I made in Photoshop. I make all my chapter titles in Photoshop and then my books are consistent between the hardcopy and the eBook. (This may be the best tip I give you, so be sure you use it to make your stuff look more professional than the competition because I don't think others are doing this.)

So I add this as a picture in the eBook for the chapter title:

CHAPTER 1

His Girl Maddie

If you are only offering a digital copy (eBook), you should still track preorders to gain insight into how effective your marketing has been. Amazon has a nice way of tracking this. You can track the preorders for your Kindle at this website kdp.amazon.com. They keep track of daily Kindle sales, as well as preorder sales. You can see in the following graph that I was selling no copies of *The Blue Rose* magazine. Then, for Amazon Prime Day, October 11th, I lowered all 15 copies of *The Blue Rose* to $2.99 an eBook. You can see the jump in sales around Prime Day. Pre-orders went up, too. (See photo on next page.)

Unfortunately, my strategy means that I forfeited a large portion of my profit. In this case, my hope was that if I could encourage people to buy Issue #4, then maybe they would want to buy #5 and so on and so on. But if you only have one eBook out, you'll have to decide if it is the right choice to give up 50% of your profit just to drive sales. Only you can answer that. I can tell you that I have plenty of data to support the

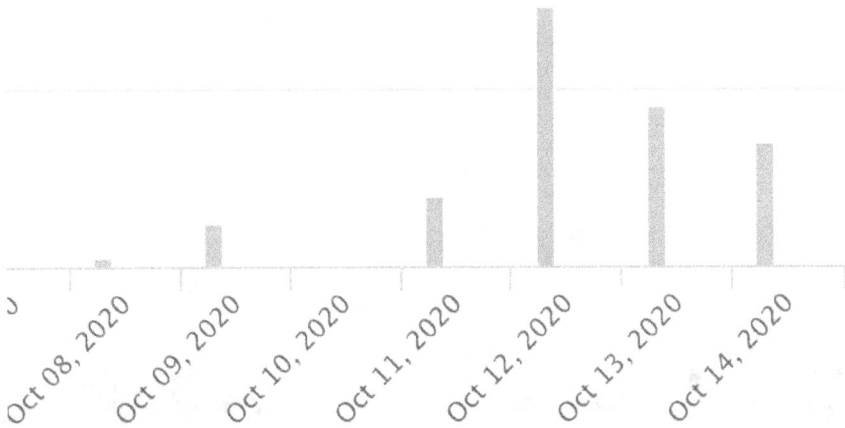

fact that people only really want to buy my products when they are sure that I am making nothing on them. They don't mind if Amazon gets money, but they really seem to hate it if me or my family have a roof over our heads. That is just the way it is for small-time authors. Embrace it, prepare for it, and price accordingly.

Chapter Takeaways

1. Find a software that works best for your needs and meets your technological know-hows (within a reasonable learning curve).

2. The eBook will have a different design than the print book, and you will not have as much control over how eReaders experience your work.

3. If you're going to take publication seriously, and especially if you intend to do more than one book, investing in Adobe programs will be the best decision you make.

CHAPTER EIGHT

What Makes a Good Book Design?

Book design is the formatting of your final manuscript. It is the interior art form of perfecting the margins, page numbers, chapter titles, and fonts. This is a critical step to finalizing your narrative and making it easy on the reader to consume.

Grab a cup of coffee, because it's about to get monotonous. Let's talk about formatting. As boring as margins, fonts, and gutters sound, they're a necessary part of the equation. They are the small details that turn a manuscript into a beautifully published work. If readers preferred narratives handwritten on crinkled paper and drenched with coffee stains, we'd be mailing each other originals. That would certainly make some lives easier. But, most consumers prefer a story tied with a bow; accessible, structured, neat and tidy. Even handwritten letters get a little more love if the margins are tight and lettering pristine. As we mentioned before, readers are used to taking narrative journeys within a familiar structure. If they purchase a book, they're going to want it to look like a book. Unless they're looking for abstract art, in which case, this is the wrong book for you to be referencing in your creative endeavors.

While your text is the ultimate journey your readers will embark upon, the layout of your book is an experience in itself. The formatting of the text indicates what kind of narrative they're reading, how much dialogue is in a scene, and which story elements are most important. Although one extra paragraph or line of white space won't change the text itself, it can influence the experience of a reader. Additionally, it is critical that others are able to follow your story without losing words in the gutter of the book or becoming distracted by poorly-placed images. Interior design can make or break a published work.

If you're not sure where to start, find yourself a bookshelf. Go to the library, a local bookshop, or your grandma's house, and start researching. Take note of what other authors and publishers have done before, and recognize which genres might follow similar patterns. If you're still lost, use your publishing platform's templates or guides. Amazon KDP, for example, provides its users a downloadable template with sample text to give you a basic concept of professional formatting. No matter which publishing platform you choose, they should tell you the margins you need and give you dimensions for the cover design.

To help make this a little more digestible, we decided to offer some bite-sized chunks:

<u>Margins</u>

Margins serve as intentional white space around the edge of your text and protects your narrative from falling too far into the gutter (middle of the book). They indicate where a line of text begins and ends, and gives the reader's eye a guide to seamlessly flow from one line of text to the next. If you are going for a professional look, be sure to justify your text so that the content reaches both the left and right margins. This may appear odd at first because of the funky spacing in between some text, but if you start to doubt this formatting standard, take another look at the books on your bookshelf. We're willing to bet they all look the same. As a reader, we rarely notice the extra space and it helps keep the margins clean and easy to follow.

•••••

Scott: Margins are so important; I feel like there is no way to overstate it. The majority of mistakes that new designers make is forgetting how much we need white space on the page. I will honestly admit that I have really struggled with this, especially in designing *The Blue Rose*. I pay, out of my pocket, for each page of that magazine, and I have always wanted to fill it to the brim. But you have to step back and let words breathe on the page. You have to leave some space around the photos and space between the captions under the photos. When it comes to designing a book, you have to remember that if your book gets long, the reader will have to pull the pages farther apart to be able to read the middle of your book. You want to be sure you have left enough room in the gutter so readers can read every word. This is something to look at when you are proofing your final document.

Chapter Titles

In addition to being concise and relevant in naming your chapter titles (you don't have to stick with, "Chapter One," "Chapter Two," etc.), be sure to format them in a way that clearly indicates a new chapter. It is not uncommon, for example, to see the first word or first letter of a chapter enlarged, with the rest of the paragraph flowing around it. The beginning of each chapter should also start at least a quarter of the way down a page and preferably on the right hand side. (Scott disagrees that it matters which side of the page your chapter begins or ends.) You can even include pictures or designs on your chapter pages, but make sure that whichever choice you make remains consistent throughout the book.

•••••

Scott: I love to have fun chapter titles. My chapter titles for *Moonlighting*, as seen in the previous chapter, are one example.. I love including some photos or pictures. In this book, we decided to use the keyboard from a computer. It is a great way to say what your book is and make the book fun as you go along. Also, be sure that if your chapters have titles, you are using consistent capitalization. Consistency is the key to book design. (See Chapter 7 for examples.)

I published a book through *The Blue Rose* called *Twin Peaks Unwrapped* by Ben Durant and Bryon Kozaczka. There have been so many *Twin Peaks* books out there, I wanted to design a fun, different chapter heading. They were covering every episode of the series. I thought using a screen capture from the series would be fun. I tried to pick something that was not prominent in the episode, and never of a person. This would be a nice deep cut for hardcore fans, which would be the primary audience for this book. Here is what I came up with:

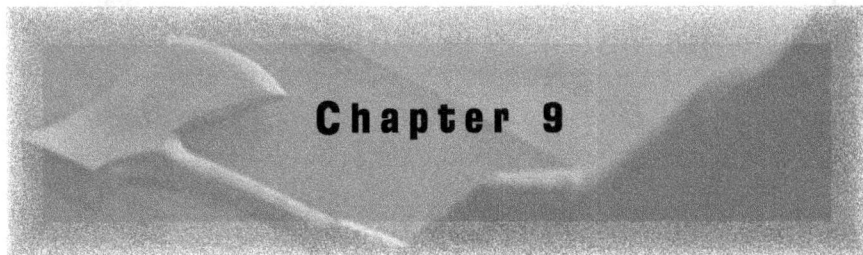

I made a fun border, picked a good shot and then a clear text for the chapter number. Any true fan of the show, would see that shot and know immediately that is from the first season finale and know that chapter is about Episode 7. Have fun with your design and put in Easter eggs for fans, when you can.

Page numbers

While you don't necessarily need a table of contents, you definitely can't have a professional-quality publication without page numbers. Speaking of your table of contents, it is common practice to use lowercase Roman numerals (i, ii, iii) instead of the normal 1, 2, 3. Additionally, it is not unusual to refrain from placing page numbers on display pages, including the copyright page, dedication, title pages, or section dividers. Blank pages should be left blank, which means omitting the page number as well. You can place page numbers wherever your heart desires but, again, maintain consistency throughout the book.

Spacing

Most books will not likely warrant creative spacing. However, especially if you have dialogue or a uniquely structured narrative, you may need to add some extra white space. The trick here is to leave enough white space to indicate the pause in narrative that you need, without leaving the reader wondering when the next line will begin. Additionally, pay attention to where your text is ending up as you format the interior of your book. Is there a single word straggling onto the next page? Is there a word change or spacing option that might resolve the issue? Be cognizant of where your white space is being implemented and how it is affecting the rest of the text.

Notice how we are consistent with spaces in the chapter sections. There is a space above and below each new section. When Erin or Scott talk, we used dots with a space above, but not below. It doesn't matter how you space, but it does matter that you are always consistent.

Indentation and Spaces

It may be tempting to hit the tab button when you start a new paragraph, so tempting that your computer may even do it for you. It's time to reprogram both you and your technology. Hitting tab will indent your paragraphs more than the standard amount for professionally published books. Instead, set the indentation in your document settings to 1.25cm. Additionally, we know that some of us (*cough* Erin *cough*) were taught to use two spaces in between sentences. Maybe when you're learning to handwrite, the two finger spaces make sense. However, not when you're writing a book. A single space is plenty to give the reader a breather. Two spaces is inefficient and looks bad to the everyday consumer.

Title pages and copyright

Inside a standard publication, there is usually a separate cover page (sometimes referred to as a half title) and a title page. The original intent behind this was to protect the actual title page from damage while delivering an unbound book from the printer to a bookbinder. Often, the half title is just as it indicates; half of the title page. It typically only has the title of the book and rarely features any unique designs or formatting. The title page has the author's name and any artwork associated with the title. It may also have the logo of the publisher. After the title is the copyright page, where you provide information about the book, including the year of publication, ISBN, publisher, any disclaimers, rights, credits, and LCCN if you have one. Standard copyright page templates can be found online or, again, wander over to that bookshelf and see what other published copies have included.

Font

Fonts are fun, but nobody wants a book written in Wingdings. Professionally published books typically stick to the classics: Garamond, Times New Roman, Baskerville, Helvetica, Caslon, or Palatino. These are the easiest fonts to read and can more reliably be printed as intended. Unless you are issuing a large font book, stick to anywhere between size 10 and 14 for the main narrative. The reason for the variance is that different fonts look better in different sizes, so you'll need to do a print test to see which combination works best. Chapter titles and other special text is, of course, up to your discretion. Just don't go wild. And no Wingdings, please. When it comes to color, black font is the classic choice. While color font is accessible, keep in mind that it may cost more to print and should be used sparingly so as not to overwhelm a reader's eyes.

Notice our use of font in this book. We used the same font for each of the chapter titles. We also used a different font for the sections within the chapters. We matched that font to the Chapter Takeaway's font. When Scott did the bit about Google Docs, and Erin "jumped in," we used a more *flowery font* for her text. But, notice that it is kind of hard to read. If we used that for the entire book, you probably would have put this down by now. (If you are still reading it by now anyway.)

Images

Images can add character to a book and provide necessary reference, depending on your subject matter. The key here is to be selective and try not to overburden your reader by requiring them to constantly navigate around pictures. Remember that photos can add bulk to a manuscript, which raises the printing cost and can therefore make it more expensive for consumers (unless you prefer to make less money per copy). Additionally, printing in color drastically increases the cost of production, so if you're going to keep costs low it's best to refrain from using too many images. Make sure the pictures you choose are high-quality and look good in grayscale (unless you're paying for color). If you have any doubts about the quality of a photo, print a sample page to see how it looks, bearing in mind the quality may still be downgraded in the print-on-demand process. Even if you love the picture, if the quality is bad, we urge you to hit "delete." No one likes a pixelated image, and if the reader can't tell what's going on, it will decrease the professionalism of your work. However you decide to put images in your book, maintain consistency and place them purposefully so that it makes sense to the reader.

Be sure to have photo credits underneath your photos. This can be tedious if your book has a ton of pictures, but it's the right thing to do. Remember that if you are doing a book that uses pop culture, publicity photos, you can use them as long as you are commenting directly on that photo. Also, if you use a photo, you need to give the photographer credit. So in Scott's *Moonlighting* book photos are listed as "Photo Courtesy of ABC Publicity." If one of the writers gave him the photo from behind the scenes, the credit read, "Photo Courtesy of Debra Frank."

Paper Color

Speaking of interior coloring, one of the decisions you will need to make with regard to production is the paper color. You typically have two options: cream and white. For context with this decision, let's imagine you've managed to reach the superior level of lounging on a sunny beach with someone assigned to provide you bottomless Mai Tais. You have a book in hand and are leisurely perusing through it. Are the pages making you squint? Do you feel as though you need a second pair of sunglasses? Our guess is the book is probably printed on white paper. This is why, most often, books are printed on cream unless they are a resource (such as a textbook) or contain color images. If your book is mostly text, and especially if it is intended for leisurely reading, cream is probably the best choice. No one likes unnecessary eye strain, especially when you're trying to figure out how Hermione is getting to class so quickly or what happened to Ron's rat.

•••••

Erin: I have understood and valued the importance of formatting since the fifth grade. Something about the pristine structure of a five-paragraph essay was, in some strange way, calming to my anxious writer's mind. As I got older and began writing research papers, although five paragraphs turned into 30 and beyond, formatting was a way to turn a jumbled mess of thoughts into an organized, easily-comprehensible story. Designing a book is no different.

I knew what I wanted to say when I sat down to write *Gui Ren*. I had a few blogs to work from and videos to help recreate vivid visuals for the reader. I also knew that, when the time came to present those stories to the world, I wanted people to take it seriously. I wanted someone to pick my book from the shelf and recognize that, although it is self-published, it meets their expectations of what a book should look and feel like. I wanted to invite them into my world by first stepping into theirs.

Take Marcel Duchamp's work of art entitled, "Fountain," for example. Had I seen a urinal sitting on the side of the highway, I would have considered it discarded trash. But, when Duchamp put it in a museum, it suddenly became art. Books tend to operate in the same way. If I would have chosen to share *Gui Ren* in a spiral bound notebook, or ignored all recommendations on margins, it may not have reached an audience looking for a good book to read. I wanted to deliver my stories in a way that met certain expectations so that I could then take them on an unexpected and compelling journey.

The art is the narrative, but having a professional book design is the first step to someone picking up your book and giving it a chance. No matter how silly or mundane it might seem to conform to society's standards of publication, getting your thoughts into the hands of readers starts with meeting them where they are: at the bookstore. And you know what most bookstores don't accept? Spiral-bound notebooks.

•••••

Scott: I have been creating art in some form or another since 1987. I always tried to create my art to mimic the credits, design and packaging of a similar piece of art that I liked. If I made a movie, I had the credits flow in the same order as my favorite movie of that time. My first movie was based on an episode of the television series *Moonlighting*. I structured that film like they did on *Moonlighting*. I made commercials to play every ten minutes. I didn't know the difference between a line producer or a director of photography, but I used those credits and made it up. (Hey, I was 17.) When I produced a CD, I had Billy Joel's *Storm Front* sitting next to mine and made sure I had the same credit styles. When it came time to write *Scott Luck Stories*, I had John Irving's essay book, *Trying to Save Piggy Sneed*, next to my computer and referenced it for inspiration. I also went to a bookstore and looked for books that were similar to mine.

The first book I designed was *The Last Days of Letterman*. It was a book about a TV show, so I went to a book store and found the section of books about television. I looked at how other authors designed their books about TV shows. It doesn't mean you have to do what they did. Sometimes, you see what someone else did and you know that you hate it. That's good. It means you have your own style. But there are certain things you want to have in your manuscript to make sure your book is taken seriously. You may get an idea by looking at someone else's design and adapting it. Meeting the standards set by published authors and designers will make your product look on par.

Chapter Takeaways

1. Your book will ultimately be judged by how you create the interior; make sure you pay close attention and are consistent throughout the design.

2. Don't be afraid of leaving blank space so the book can breathe.

3. Never use a photo that will print poorly and always credit the photographer; make sure you have permission to use the photo.

CHAPTER NINE

What About ISBNs, Barcodes, and Copyrights?

International Standard Book Numbers (ISBN) are thirteen-digit identification numbers that are used for listing and managing book sales. This is a critical number for booksellers, libraries, publishers, and internet retailers to be able to locate, list, and distribute your title. An ISBN gives your book a specific number that will be attached to it across the globe. It means there will be no confusion about which book is yours. As an example, let's say you have creatively decided to call your book The Promise. Well, there is a really good chance there are several other books with that same title as well. But there can be only one book that has your unique ISBN. Additionally, if you write sequels, the ISBN will differentiate each book in that series.

Every product in the world has its own version of an ISBN attached to it. From your vacuum cleaner to your latest Jawa action figure. If it has a name, and it's for sale, it has a number. Your book needs one as well. You can easily buy an ISBN at www.myidentifiers.com. But wait, before you put this book down and whip out your credit card, there is a big decision to make, and only you can make it. How many ISBNs should you buy? We'll let you in on a secret: The more you buy, the cheaper they are. Of course, the more you buy, the more you will spend at once. But, in the long run, that may be worth the investment. Let's take a look at why.

The pricing for ISBNs is kind of crazy. Here is the pricing as of October 2020:

- To buy 1 ISBN is $125 [$125 per ISBN]
- To buy 10 ISBNs is $295 [$29.50 per ISBN]
- To buy 100 ISBNs is $575 [$5.75 per ISBN]

You can see how quickly that price moved down. Because ISBNs are unique identifiers, each edition and variation of your work will need its own number. This includes paperbacks, eBooks, audio books, and hardcover editions. Are you going to just write one book? Well, even if you write one, you might need two ISBNs; one for the print copy and one for the eBook. Are you doing an audio book as well? Guess what, you already need three. And this was only one project. What are your future plans? Do you think you are going to do 4 projects over your lifetime? If so, 100 might be the best value because buying 20 ISBNs is going to cost you $600.

Important note: Amazon provides free ISBNs. However, as with most things on Amazon, it comes at a cost. If you use one of Amazon's free ISBNs when publishing your print-on-demand title, you do not maintain full rights to your published work. Instead, the print-on-demand service gets to list themselves, and in Amazon's case, Independently Published, as the publisher. Additionally, and perhaps most importantly, using Amazon's ISBN means the book can only be published and distributed by Amazon. You would not be allowed to take your title to another self-publishing service like IngramSpark or BookBaby. So, if you want to be listed as the publisher and maintain full ownership over your work, buy your own ISBN.

•••••

Scott: I bought one ISBN when I published *Scott Luck Stories* in 2014 because I thought I would never publish anything again. I have since published 15 magazines and 10 books, so I was dumb. When I started FMP with David Bushman, we didn't even discuss it. I said, "We are buying 100 ISBNs." We are still using them in the third year of our company and probably will never use them all, but who knows. The cost was much cheaper per book to do it that way.

•••••

Erin: I bought one ISBN for *Gui Ren* and then immediately regretted my decision. Although I didn't have any concrete future book ideas, I suddenly realized how likely it was that I would need another ISBN and began to recognize just how crappy of a value I was getting for just one. So, I ended up contacting Bowker and requesting a refund because (silly me) I should have invested in the 10 pack from the start. They graciously issued a one-time reversal and permitted me to purchase the 10 pack. I have since used eight of those ISBNs, only two being my own works. Maybe Scott will let me steal some of his when I run out … (**Scott:** I will trade ISBNs for cookies.)

Pricing Your Book

In order to complete the set up for your ISBN, you'll need to decide a list price. This is another time in which some extra research will definitely come in handy. Start by looking at other recent titles for sale within your genre and compare various elements such as the number of pages, trim size, whether the book is in color, and how many images are included. Remember that production costs can influence the list price, so bear that in mind as you're assessing the titles on your bookshelf. The key here is not to price too low, but also not to make people grip onto their credit cards for fear that you might outright rob them. It's all a balance. Maximize your net profit while acknowledging what a fair market price might be for the title you're trying to sell.

•••••

Scott: Pricing a book can be such a tricky thing to do. First of all, you are not going to recoup all the time, energy, heart, and hard work you put into the book with the retail price you slap on the back cover of your book. If that were the case, I would have listed *Moonlighting: An Oral History* at the low, low cost of $185.99 a copy. Instead I priced the print book at $29.99 and the eBook at $11.99. That is a pricey book, but let me walk you through why I priced it the way I did.

The book is in full color, which made the printing cost per book go up $2 a book. A book about television would more likely be priced at $24.99. My distributor would really want me to price it at $19.99, but the pricing margins start getting too small. Also, this is the first book about *Moonlighting* ever to be written, which means there isn't competition out there. Cybill Shepherd is in the book; that is some star power and worth raising the price $5. But, remember, since I am not self-publishing my books, I will only get half the money to begin with. My distributor sells the books at 50% off to Amazon, Barnes & Noble and all bookstores, so it already starts out at $14.99 profit for me. Then, my distributor takes 25% of that. We are now down to $11.24. I also have to pay to print 3,000 copies of the book out of my pocket. I also have to pay for editing, design, cover design and I have a partner. When you start dividing out all those costs, you can see why I thought this book should be $29.99.

When I wrote *Scott Luck Stories*, which was an eBook only, I priced it at $3.99. No one knew who I was, no one was going to want to buy this book, and I knew I had to price it low. Amazon takes 35% of the revenue. I recently did a historical search on the book. It was released October 31, 2016. Today is October 25, 2020. So, it's been 4 years. I have made $151 in profit over those 4 years. That is $37.50 a year. Wow, you can see how rich I have become from writing. It isn't easy to make a splash in the self-publishing game. Let's not forget I paid $125 for an ISBN number, so you subtract that from the $151 and you basically get a Wendy's 4 for 4. (I suggest a Junior Bacon, Nuggets, and fries and swap out the drink for a vanilla Frosty.)

All in all, you will need to balance your expenses when deciding a price, but also, understand that you are probably not going to make up all those beginning costs (think Adobe Photoshop, InDesign, etc.). Make the investment wisely, but know it is just that: an investment. Self-publishing gives you a leg up on making money, so don't sell yourself short by underpricing your work. If you're going to do that, you may as well go with a traditional publisher.

•••••

Erin: When it came time to price *Gui Ren*, I sat down at my computer and typed, "*Eat, Pray, Love*" into Amazon's search bar. I had read somewhere that you should compare your book to other titles in the genre and base your own price off of books of similar length. While that's not a terrible place to start, keep in mind that sellers will list a book at different prices depending on supply and demand. So, first of all, you can't take the price at face value. Secondly, the amount of time that a book has been on the market can influence the price. Finally, depending on how you intend to print and distribute your book, pricing lower may lessen your chances of breaking even, let alone making a profit.

What's my point in all this rambling? Do the research, but trust your instinct. *Eat, Pray, Love* is currently listed at $12.16 on Amazon. I priced *Gui Ren* at $17.95. Why? Because I wanted to. Plain and simple as that. With just over 350 pages filled with riveting adventures and self-discovery, I felt it was worth that and then some. And, you know what? People bought it. At the end of the day, the price shouldn't make a difference if your promotional efforts are effective. Besides, *Eat, Pray, Love* was published in 2006. I think thirteen years might warrant a different assessment of monetary value. Pricing my book at $17.95 and ordering author copies to resell through my own channels meant I was averaging about $8.50 profit per book (including Amazon sales). Nothing Mai Tai worthy, but just enough to break even.

The best advice I can give you is don't price too low (you shouldn't completely be robbed of printing fees), and don't price too high—$75 for a 150-page biography about your cat is unlikely to sell (unless you're already rich and famous, in which case, why in the world are you self-publishing?). I mean, I'm all for independence and DIY, but I'd probably hire someone else to do parts of the self-publishing process for me if I could afford it. Ask Scott, he's already on my payroll. Fortunately, he accepts cookies.

Barcodes

The barcode located at the bottom of the back cover is one of those little things that makes your design look professional and functional. A barcode allows a retail store to scan the barcode and the ISBN number to check the price and track store sales and inventory.

•••••

Scott: Nothing will make you happier than seeing that your book looks like every professionally published book you have ever seen. Recently, a friend of mine asked if I would offer advice to someone who was publishing their first book. The writer told me a local store wasn't willing to sell their comic books because there was no barcode for them to scan. They said they knew there was no way they could get a barcode made without having a real publisher. This blew me away. For all the things that should stop you from getting your work out into the world, the barcode is the last thing.

Now, the internet is an ever-changing beast. Websites appear and disappear all the time. However, at the time of publishing this book, you could generate a free barcode for your ISBN at: online-barcode-generator.net/.

If, for some reason, this website is no longer accessible (what a shame that would be), you can pay Bowker (www.myidentifiers.com/) $25 for a barcode. There is no difference in the usefulness of the barcode.

When you create your barcode you will enter in how much the cover price of your book is, and it spits out something that looks like this:

ISBN 9781733338080   51499 >

9 781733 338080

This barcode lists the ISBN: 9781733338080 and then the code: 51499. The "5" in that second number indicates the book is printed and priced in The United States of America. The 1499 represents the price $14.99, which is the cover price of the book. All of that data is encoded in the barcode. When generating your own barcode, just click "give me my barcode," and it will automatically download a PDF and EPS of the barcode.

If you are like Erin, (who doesn't want to be just like Erin?) and you want the price presented more clearly so customers can easily locate the exact price, you can load the file into Adobe Photoshop and add the text: US Retail Price: $14.99 above the 51499.

As you can see, this may very well be the easiest thing you do when you create your entire book. Obtaining a barcode shouldn't be daunting, so don't let that stop you from creating a book with a professional look.

Copyright and Trademark

We're going to give you a brief overview of copyright and trademark within the context of self-publishing, but to fully understand how to protect your work and/or your business entities, please consult with an attorney. We are not here to give legal advice; we are simply sharing our own opinions, experiences, and most basic knowledge. Know that our opinions or recommendations may not be right for you and your creative work. We will not be held responsible for whichever path you choose.

Now that the boring disclaimers are covered, let's resume. You have a great story to tell, and you're excitedly sharing the premise with the world, so there might be something quite important nagging you: copyright. Of course you are protective of your creative work and you don't want anyone else to profit from your efforts. But, how necessary is registering with the U.S. Copyright Office?

Let's first understand what constitutes copyright infringement. According to copyright.gov, "copyright infringement occurs when a copyrighted work is reproduced, distributed, performed, publicly displayed, or made into a derivative work without the permission of the copyright owner." Explicitly, if you use someone else's ideas or original work, and especially if you claim them as your own or fail to give credit, you are in dangerous territory, friend. You are cruisin' for a bruisin'.

You can't copyright an idea, so until your work is in tangible form, it is not protected. Once in physical form, your work serves as proof of concept or originality. Should you end up in court over copyright infringement, you can use that to prove first conceptualization and to indicate the similarities between works. While your written work does not need to be published in order to be protected by copyright, registering will strengthen your case with a legally upstanding date of originality.

The commonly known "poor man's copyright" (mailing yourself and keeping a sealed copy of your manuscript) may hold up in court, but it is definitively not as supportive as a registration with the U.S. Copyright Office. If you are really concerned about someone stealing your work, you can timestamp your drafts, send copies to trusted families and friends as evidence, or mail yourself a sealed copy, but know that the best way to truly protect your work is to register it.

With copyright infringement in mind, you also have a responsibility to abide by the framework that applies to you as a creative. Just as you don't want other people stealing your ideas, don't be that person to someone else. Do not use song lyrics, quotes, content, or reproduced work without written permission from the original artist or author. Why written? Because verbal agreements are pretty difficult to prove in court.

•••••

Scott: I use a Sondheim song lyric in each of my books. I pick one that reflects my time working on that particular book. But I only pick a couplet. You can have free use as long as you sight the author and where it is from. If it is within the context of an essay, footnote it. You can use a screen capture from a pop culture motion picture or TV program as long as you directly mention the photo within your text. So I can use a screen capture from a *Moonlighting* episode to show readers which scene I am discussing, but I can't just use a photo from the show and not mention it or not have it reflected in my writing. Promotional photos can only be used for journalism and critical analysis. These are all the things you need to worry about if you are using someone else's art to express your own thoughts. For example, you can use promotional photos for an album, TV show, or film, but you cannot use an individual's art or photos without written permission from them or the organization. Think of it this way, if someone wants to quote your book in their book, you will want the credit as well. So always be sure to cite, footnote, and acknowledge your source material.

•••••

Erin: As soon as I had a nearly completed draft, I used the "poor man's copyright" for *Gui Ren* with the understanding that while it may not protect me in a court of law, it could be proof enough to insert doubt into a legal case. However, the nature of my work was nonfiction, so the likelihood of someone stealing my idea and replicating my stories were slim. They would have had to use my blog posts and pictures in order to formulate a narrative that looked anything like my original experiences, so the risk would be far too high for any one (sane) person.

•••••

Plainly put, registering your copyright gives further strength to taking someone to court and collecting damages. There is a reason every professionally produced literary work has a copyright page; it is the location in which you indicate ownership and declare your rights as the author of the original work. You might see phrases such as "All rights reserved" or "No part of this book may be reproduced." You will also likely see the copyright symbol © and publication date or date of conception.

Then, there are trademarks. These are registered elements of branding that represent goods or services and differentiate them from other similar products. Generally, a book title cannot be trademarked, but something like a logo, slogan, or symbol can be. Heck, you can even trademark a color and scent. So, go nuts. While a book title itself can't be trademarked, a series title could because it is considered a form of branding. For example, if your branding extends beyond the title of the book and incorporates an all-encompassing business plan or product line for *A Deer at the Feeder* as a concept, trademarking your materials may be wise. The underlying recommendation is, if your book becomes a brand, or your branding results in a book, you should be sure that branding is protected. Trademarking might also be a consideration if, like Erin, you set up an LLC under which to publish your book.

•••••

Erin: When I began writing *Gui Ren*, I knew I would be unapologetically telling the full story, good or bad. Because it was nonfiction, however, and there were real people behind every story, I thought it was appropriate to take certain precautions. Although the stories I shared were true, "truth" can be subjective, and therefore an individual could claim libel under the right circumstances. R is one of the primary characters in my story, but had I published his actual name or company, I knew he would have every right to sue for defamation. So, naturally, I did everything I could to make my intentions clear. I added a disclaimer to the beginning of my work in which I state that these experiences are solely my own perspective and I changed some names out of respect for those individuals' privacy. I never shared R's actual name or company, whether in the book or during public presentations about my journey. And I started an LLC for the publishing company that was listed as my imprint: Fishtail Publishing. Therefore, my personal assets would be protected. Fortunately, this has never been an issue, but it sure as heck was a peace of mind for me when hitting publish. Considering how Fishtail Publishing has evolved into a fully functioning business, it was a great move for me and my career. (P.S. Fishtail Publishing is a result of one 9-year-old's dream to one day run a publishing company. If you haven't read the "about us" section at fishtailpublishing.org, check it out. It's pretty adorable.)

I did consider putting a trademark on the artwork on my front cover and the phrase *Gui Ren* as it continued to serve business purposes outside of the book. I started a social media campaign geared toward collecting stories of *Gui Ren*, used the concept in educational programming for student storytellers, and based my own storytelling performances around this phrase. It was quickly becoming a branding tool for my work. However, as I began the process, I learned that in order to truly get the most security or value out of trademarking, I would have to regularly monitor the international businessphere to ensure no one was inappropriately utilizing my marks. That's right, just because you have a trademark doesn't mean the government has your back. They're not scrounging the internet on your behalf looking for thieves. They'll only really have your back if you present a problem to them and, even then, they're only as good as the information they have. If you catch someone utilizing your trademark, you're still responsible for hiring an attorney, presenting a case, settling, and losing what is probably valuable work time in the process. Don't get me wrong, there's value in trademarking and there's value in protecting your assets. I won't deny that. However, as one of the smallest fish in the sea with little-to-no chances of a multi-million dollar enterprise based on *Gui Ren*, I opted to take my chances.

Beyond the fact that I couldn't see myself monitoring the interwebs or being upset that someone thought my idea was cool, the most prominent reason for tossing the application was that the nature of *Gui Ren* is to connect and inspire. It is an embracing and supporting concept of character and humanism. I believe in the concept far more than I believe in the ownership of it. In fact, ownership—in my mind—would kind of defeat the purpose. So, I decided it best existed unclaimed[1]. If you feel so inclined to copy my untrademarked mark and turn *Gui Ren* into a multi-million dollar enterprise, by all means. Forge ahead. But, at least offer me a management position. It would be the respectful thing to do.

Library of Congress Control Number (LCCN)

There are quite a few opinions about whether or not a Library of Congress Control Number (LCCN) is necessary or worth it. But, it's free (sort of), easy to do, and could increase your chances of being taken seriously by local libraries across the country. As an author, you would apply for a pre-publication LCCN that acts as a tracking number for your title and lets the Library of Congress know to expect an incoming submission. The identification number provided serves to catalogue your book in their independent database of literature. Once published and printed, you ship them a copy for review and hope they add it to their collection. If they do, they will provide the Cataloging-in-Publication (CIP) data that would tell libraries where to shelve the title according to the Dewey Decimal Classification, which, if you know anything about libraries, you know that's pretty basic information to provide should they have requests to carry your title.

CIP data, in general, makes it easier for people to find your book, particularly when searching for subjects on a library's website. So, you can see why it might be beneficial. While you can still obtain CIP data without going through the Library of Congress, applying for an LCCN is free (minus the cost of shipping them a copy) and fairly quick to do. It can't hurt, and if you want libraries to take you seriously, it's certainly

---

1.   I am still protected, to a certain extent, by the copyright of my book and dated proof of concept. With the right attorney, should a case arise, I would still have reasonable ground to stand on.

worth the extra effort. All that being said, Erin does it for herself and her clients, and Scott doesn't. Like we said, differing opinions.

Chapter Takeaways

1. You need an ISBN no matter what, so you may as well ensure that you retain control of your title; buy your own and consider buying more than one at a time.

2. If you're considering registering a copyright or trademark, do your own research and consult with an attorney to determine whether or not it's the right path for you. It may not be worth the investment.

3. There are several ways to further validate your work other than by simply hitting "publish," but that doesn't mean you have to take advantage of every option for your work to be considered professional and legitimate. Most of that will be determined by the look and feel of your title.

CHAPTER TEN

What Else Do I Need?

After almost 100 pages, you would think you know it all. (And if you are one of Scott's teenagers, then you definitely think you know it all.) There are so many little factors in birthing a book to the world. We tried to combine as many as we could into this catch all chapter. We apologize because while we wrote it we were listening to the movie soundtrack from the Broadway show *Chicago*.

"I Can't Do it Alone"

Scott: One of the myths of being a writer is that it is an individual activity. Just like Catherine Zeta-Jones's character in the film *Chicago*—you can't do it alone. When it comes to setting words down in a Google doc (or if you are old, on paper), you will complete that task alone. Even this book, which Erin and I wrote at the very same time—she worked on one section while I worked on another section as we sat across from each other in Panera or over Zoom (Damn you, pandemic!)—the writing still happened alone. But an author can only thrive when they have a peer group.

I am sure that somewhere out there is some writer (probably Ken Follett, that prolific jerk) who can just happily write, edit, and publish in a room by himself. But most of us need to see others and interact with others to know that a task can be accomplished. Completing your first book is an amazing accomplishment. It makes it so much easier if you have a friend, colleague, or even a stranger, to walk alongside you. Now, let's make a few things clear before we go too far. I am not saying that this is someone who you go to the local coffee shop and get a danish with and don't do any writing while you take up a table as college kids glare at you. That's called having lunch with a friend. (Damn you, pandemic!) I am talking about a colleague who inspires you, helps you when you have questions, or, on the flip side, a nemesis who challenges you and maybe even lights a fire under you as you watch them rise to the top.

For me, I found this community by going to the *Twin Peaks* Festival in Snoqualmie, Washington in 2015. I met so many friends, and almost all of them were artists of some kind. I met people who were writers (published or bloggers), I met podcasters (who doesn't have a podcast by now?), painters, poets, wood workers, and jewelry makers. Seeing all these people who were creating art AND putting it out into the world for money made me realize it was time to get serious. If you are following my timeline, you will know that in 2015 I had already published my eBook, *Scott Luck Stories*. So, I was a writer, but I wasn't prolific, and I wasn't pushing myself. Meeting someone like Brad Dukes, the author of *Reflections: An Oral History of Twin Peaks*, really inspired me to start writing about television.

Brad Dukes was a fan of *Twin Peaks*, but had never published a major book about the subject. He started reaching out to the cast and getting interviews. Over five years he continued to do this. He compiled these interviews into a book and released it on his own through Amazon. (See our Appendix for more on Brad.) He got a bit of luck when, one week after his book was released, *Twin Peaks* released a new box set with deleted scenes that had never been seen before. He couldn't have planned the timing, but because he followed his passion and crafted a book about a TV show that hadn't made news for twenty years, he had a product to coincide with this moment. Since then, his book has been translated into several languages and is listed alongside books about *Twin Peaks* that were released by the show runners themselves. Follow your passion, get in a peer group, be inspired and become inspiring for someone else. Watching Brad do what he did made it much easier for me to write my *thirtysomething* book because I had seen a friend do a similar product.

Years later, when he was working on a book about *China Beach*, he mentioned how I had inspired him. This came as a shock because he was such a mentor to me. We had only met three times at different *Twin Peaks* events. But a lifelong friendship formed because of our passion for writing about television. I could tell a similar story about eight or nine other friends whom I met over the last five years, including Courtenay Stallings, who edited this very book. Courtenay was the one who invited me to that festival. Now she is my editor. Meeting other artists is key. Before 2015, I knew no one who wrote or designed books. Be open to new friends and their experiences because I promise you'll inspire and encourage each other. Soon … you'll go. Then they'll go. Then we'll go. But you can't do it alone.

•••••

Erin: I couldn't possibly have written *Gui Ren* and known how to go about self-publishing without the support, enthusiasm, and guidance from others around me. That being said, since Scott covered the whole, "You need people thing," I'm here to remind you that you also can't take in too many voices at once. Like any major life decision or project, everyone has their own opinion. Not all of those opinions are going to resonate with you as an artist, but when asked, all of those opinions are going to make themselves heard. Here's a rule of thumb: make a short list of 3 to 5 people whose opinions matter most to you and your work. Ignore every other voice who's not on that list. Otherwise, you might become burdened by the overpowering noise of too many perspectives. At the end of the day, your art is your art, and, while getting input from others can be valuable and even encouraging, don't allow it to keep you from moving forward.

My mom will forever remind me that I should have put pictures in *Gui Ren*, "You're sharing so many adventures that you have photos of; people need to see those! It gives context! It makes a travel book more engaging!" Instead, I felt the words would be more powerful without imagery. If my narrative failed to paint a picture for a reader, that would have been the bummer, not the lack of photos. I strongly felt photos would detract from my story and lock readers into a visual world they couldn't immediately connect to. I wanted them to perceive themselves in my shoes; as soon as I introduce hard proof that the story isn't theirs, it breaks down the experience. Besides, pictures would have been more expensive to print. #NoThanksMom. My mom's opinion has been and will always be very important to me, but I had a deeply held value in my decision and did not let it change the outcome of my work. Keep your requests for input limited, know which aspects of your art are non-negotiable, and don't let the voices around you drown out what you know to be authentic and true to yourself as an artist.

P.S. Don't worry, Mom, you're still on my shortlist. Always will be.

"When you're Good To Mama"

Another benefit to knowing other people who are doing what you want to do is the professional connection. When your book is done, you better find yourself booked on podcasts that are covering the topic you wrote about it. The best way to make that happen is to start following people who have a podcast. Comment on their show. Make a connection online. Start retweeting other authors. Send them messages letting them know how much you like their work. You need a coalition to spread the word of your book. We don't know how many new self-published books are released every day on Amazon, but we are going to guess about 300,345 books a day. If you are only a drip in the splash of 300,345 books, you need to stand out. So, you need to be good to other authors so they will be good to you.

•••••

Scott: I know what you are thinking. We promised you our origin story, and you are still waiting. Here it goes. Erin and I met at Panera in 2019. We were in line for free coffee like all good writers should be. Somehow we started talking about how we were both authors who were trying to get our books into the Columbus area bookstores. Erin mentioned she was doing a book signing at a local Barnes & Noble for the unpronounceable title of her book, *Gui Ren*. She told me it was the upcoming Saturday. My wife and I showed up to the event and bought a copy. I also offered to take a picture of her when she was selling a book to a customer so she could post it on social media. We hadn't become friends yet, but it was

Erin & Scott meeting at Panera in 2019.

all about making the connection and helping her at her signing. I had been to my own book signings and knew that some go well and some don't. They are always scary to do. Having a friendly face always makes someone feel better. When you're good to Mama, Mama's good to you.

•••••

Erin: I guess what we've all learned here today is that Scott is really only friends with me because he thinks I can offer him some level of success. Well, the joke is on him. I'm just here for the packs of Chips Ahoy he sneaks into Panera. When Scott and I met that fateful day, I saw an opportunity to, one, be genuinely entertained for the entirety of whatever our relationship came to be and, two, gain further knowledge about the publishing industry. When I mentioned my book signing at Barnes & Noble, I truly didn't expect him to show up. I mean, he'd already seen the book, heard its origin stories; who would want to do that twice? Yet, he was there. And I tell you what, it did make all the difference.

I was new to the experience of trying to sell books at a table that confronted people as soon as they walked through the door of their local bookstore. It was intimidating, and I was pretty sure no one would care. And, honestly, not a lot of people did. In fact, the guy who Scott so thoughtfully took a photo of standing near my table held the book for only one moment [see photo] before requesting directions to the bathroom. He then reappeared a few short minutes later as he left the store. He wasn't even at Barnes & Noble for Barnes & Noble, let alone *Gui Ren*. The beautiful thing was, my followers didn't need to know that. All they saw was someone interested in what I had to share—even if it was a fleeting moment. I could still post that picture with an intentional caption like, "Successful day at the local Barnes & Noble connecting with readers!" and no one would know the difference. Ah, the misleading narrative of social media. But, sometimes in order to be successful, you have to pretend like you already are.

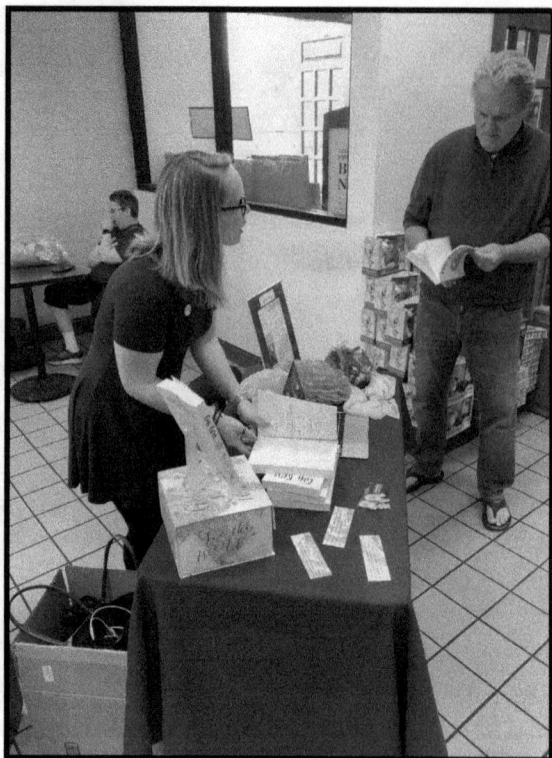

I appreciated Scott's presence at my book signing for multiple reasons. First, it gave passersby permission to approach me rather than feel intimidated by having to start the conversation themselves. Often, I find that is the most excruciating part about book signings. Second, Scott showing up reinforced that taking the first steps toward fulfilling your goals can be difficult, but is far less difficult when supported by those who genuinely believe in you. Scott has been a constant source of enthusiasm, encouragement, and reassurance throughout our friendship thus far. (**Scott:** Notice she said "thus far." She is totally expecting me to drop the ball eventually.) We lean on each other for guidance when one of us doesn't know how to get something done, and we promote one another's successes. At the end of the day, even if no one else in the world cared about my writing, I know Scott does. Or, at least, he's really good at pretending he does so I'll keep posting about his latest publication. Who cares? I'm here for the cookies, anyway.

"Razzle Dazzle"

Scott: We spent a lot of time talking about writing and design because that is such a huge part of it, but none of it matters if your work doesn't get out to the public. You can use your social media all you want, but it is really hard to get out of your circle and that is what you need to do to be self sustaining. So, what is the answer? Well, if you can get Kim Kardashian to share your book that would be great, but my guess is you don't know her. So, what is left? Well, what about hiring a publicist to give 'em the old razzle dazzle?

When I started FMP and was launching *The Last Days of Letterman*, my partner and I decided to hire a publicist to promote the book. We knew we had a great title, but we had to get the idea out there. A publicist actually ended up contacting me and asked to represent me. She had heard about the book because she was the publicist for Paul Shaffer, Letterman's band leader. How could I say no? She knew so much about Letterman and had contacts within the staff. We signed up with her. We paid her $10,000, and we knew the money would pour in. Well, it didn't pour in, it poured out.

In 6 months of representation she got me 1 interview, 1 small piece on a PBS station outside of New York, and 1 radio tour. That was it. No print articles, no podcasts, no TV appearances, and I couldn't even get Paul Shaffer to help promote the book. I basically paid her $10,000 for nothing. Adding that cost to the overall cost of printing the book made sure that even though the book sold over 4,000 copies, we would never make a profit because the cost for printing the book was over $16,000 to begin with. Now, we were getting that overall cost up to $26,000 before we even got started. Remember that our share of the profit starts at half the cover price, and then our distributor is going to take 25% on top of that. It gets to be an expensive racket. If you don't do press, you can't get the word out, and then no one buys the book. It is all a balance. In the end, we just picked a bad person. We should have put some minimums in the contract saying that some goals had to be hit for payment.

For the most part, you can book yourself on podcasts, and try to get on local radio. I am not sure the cost of a publicist can ever really be recovered in one book. You may just have to do the razzle along with the dazzle.

•••••

Erin: I'm pretty sure my childhood could be tracked via *The Columbus Dispatch*. I grew up with a parent who never hesitated to contact the local press any and every time I did something neat. Talk about Razzle Dazzle. That's not to say every article was printed, or even written for that matter, but my mom never hesitates to shout my accomplishments from the top of a mountain. Every small success elates her. My theatrical performances and volunteer efforts often ended up in the public light one way or another, whether the newspaper was searching for a fresh story or my mom sent an email. In my adolescent world, that was the way young people were rewarded for their work; memorialized in papers that would end up in every boomer parent's plastic keepsake bins for when the kids went out into the world and needed the reminder of every participation trophy and certificate of "cleanest classroom desk." I have several of those keepsake bins. Somehow, my second grade awards of participation continue multiplying.

It may not shock you, therefore, to learn the first place I went with the announcement of my book was the local newspaper (with the enthusiastic support of my mom, of course). I did a couple interviews, shared a headshot, and some Canva-designed graphics, and reposted the digital articles on all of my social media platforms. I approached the library branches that I frequented growing up and offered to do a presentation in coordination with my book release. I reached out to the local Starbucks where I composed most of my manuscript and spent countless hours with my editor; they agreed to let me do a signing. But don't be fooled, this is not to say I was always welcomed or celebrated. In fact, I sent press releases to both of my alma maters, assuming they would be most thrilled at the news, and neither one of them cared. Sometimes it's the people we anticipate will care the most who break our heart a little when they couldn't seem to be bothered. But, you try, try again. Be persistent, be proud, and shout it from the mountains. Someone will notice, someone will care, and someone will take you up on your offer to share your work with the community. If you have to create your own Razzle Dazzle, go all in. What have you got to lose?

"And All That Jazz"

Nothing in life is complete without the extra bit of Razzle Dazzle and some good old fashioned Jazz hands. Here are some other things to think about that you might have to take care of depending on how you end up running your business. We just want to throw out these ideas to try to get your brain going. Reading these all at once might be a bit overwhelming, but remember, if we can do it, you can do it.

Get a website to sell your books: Why get your own website when Amazon, Book Baby or whoever you print with can sell the book? Well, if you buy the book with your author discount from the printer/publisher and sell it on your website, you will get that extra money. You make your money in dimes, not dollars, when you are an author, so every dime helps. Also, when you sell to someone you can collect that reader's email address. That means you can directly sell to your fans and continue marketing to them when you come out with new content. Also, you could start a blog for free and bring in readers from that, then sell them your book at the bottom of the page.

Scott hosts the *Red Room Podcast*, and those episodes are uploaded to iTunes to download. But they can also be heard at his website ScottRyanProductions.com. At the bottom of every post, Scott suggests one of his books to buy that ties to the episode. Most people who click on the link just want to hear the interview with the *Twin Peaks* star whom he is interviewing, but you want to have as many chances to sell your book as possible. Here is what the post looks like at the website. This one was an interview with Sheryl Lee and Courtenay Stallings about *Laura's Ghost* which is published by FMP:

Press Play below to listen or head out to iTunes and download.

You can order the book Here.

184 Laura's Ghost with Sheryl Lee and Courtenay Sta...
on Updated 6 months ago.

More Episodes   67:51

Also be sure to subscribe to the Blue Rose Magazine Issue 14 for more Twin Peaks coverage.

Taking payments on your website: If you are going to run your website, you are going to have to take payments. This means setting up accounts with PayPal, SquareSpace, Apple Pay or some other type of online payment. Remember, they are going to take a percentage, so figure that into your cost. PayPal is the easiest, and you do not have to pay for a secure site because your customer can checkout with PayPal and use a credit or debit card, and you don't have to take the responsibility of keeping those numbers. The bad part of PayPal is they will not refund their fees. So, if your customer buys a book and then asks for their money back, you can't just refund them and PayPal gives the fee back; they keep it. So you either have to refund your customer less than they paid, or lose money and pay that fee out of your pocket. I have called and complained, but PayPal is a big company, and, therefore, doesn't offer customer service nor care if someone like me doesn't like their policy. They know I have no other option but to offer PayPal. The moment I can drop them, I will. They also won't care about that small drop off of my sales. It's just part of doing business. This goes back to the idea don't try to change the world when you're small potatoes. Just do the best you can today.

Set up an author page on Amazon: One of the features Amazon provides is letting authors set up a page that contains all their work. You can sign up as an author and then claim your books. This allows your name to be a hyperlink on the sales page. The reason this is a benefit is when a reader buys one of your books, they can easily find all of your books. Here is the link to Scott's page at www.amazon.com/-/e/B00P57Z0VM.

Customers can get to your readers page from the listing for your book on Amazon. On the previous graphic you can see how Scott's name is a blue link and allows readers to find out the other books he has written.

Set up a page on Goodreads: Goodreads is a free website that allows you to connect with readers. You can load any book that has an ISBN. It doesn't matter if you self-publish or not. If you have an ISBN, you can list it, and you should. You upload the cover, description, and fill out this form:

It is a very simple and effective way to connect with readers. You can do giveaways, contests, and pay to promote your book. The great thing about this site is that it is populated by people who like to read. So, it is a great way to make some noise and get your book out. Make sure you suggest your book to all your friends and ask people on your social media to mark your book as "to read." This then shows up in all their friends' newsfeeds. Here is the link to our book—mark it as to read to help us out, and we will do the same for you—www.goodreads.com/book/show/56757551-but-couldn-t-i-do-that.

Add a New Book

Note: Goodreads has over 12 million books in its database already, so please do a search before adding a book, as it may be a duplicate. Please also carefully read the guidelines to the right, espec the part about what kind of books to add.

title *	But, Couldn't I Do that?: Answering Your Questions About Self Publish
sort by title *	
author *	Scott Ryan Add Role
	Add new author
isbn	9781733338080 isbn 13 Click for ASIN
publisher	Fishtail Publishing LLC
published	year: 2021 month: May ▾ day: 15 ▾
number of pages	100
format	Paperback ▾ Other

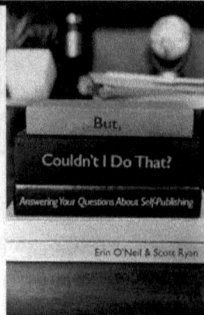

But, Couldn't I Do That?: Answering Your Questions About Self Publishing

by Erin O'Neil, Scott Ryan (Goodreads Author)

★★★★★ 0.00 · Rating details · 0 ratings · 0 reviews

How do I get my book out to the world? Which program should use to design a book? How do I make an eBook? How can I use social media to sell copies? Do I need an ISBN? What is an LCCN

<u>Chapter Takeaways</u>

1. We need each other; be good to others, and they'll (hopefully) be good to you, too. Be open-minded and willing to learn from everyone because you never know who you might meet while waiting in line for coffee.

2. Be wary of highering a publicist. Be sure you get in writing a few goals they promise to achieve.

3. Use the free ways of promoting your book like Amazon Author Pages and Goodreads.

Can You Tell Me One More Time?

Have a strong idea.

Have your concept planned out, the right social media to market it, and the skill set to be an authority on the topic. Know how to tell a quality narrative and engage readers in your particular subject matter. Get it all down on paper and finish the idea. Then, start telling everyone you know.

Decide who you want to print your work.

Pick a distributor such as Amazon, BookBaby, IngramSpark, or another platform. Know the requirements and output of each company. Be prepared to make tough decisions about where you'd like to see your book sold and how it's going to get there.

Design a captivating cover.

Do not be afraid to hire an outside specialist to design the cover for you. It is probably the best option. If you design your cover, make it simple, clear and professional. Be sure the text pops and is very readable. Check other covers from similar books and see how your book compares. Use programs like Photoshop or Illustrator to take your design and editing accessibility to the next level.

Promote, promote, promote!

You can't sell a book if people don't know it exists. Promoting your title in advance to finishing the manuscript will give you a head start on sales and audience engagement. Plus, it never hurts to give yourself a publishing deadline to keep your progress on track.

Select software that meet your publishing needs.

You might be able to get by on Microsoft Word and Google Docs for writing your manuscript, but cover design and interior formatting will require more efficient programs. Understand the differences between each of the available software and select the one that meets your publishing and budgetary needs. When in doubt, don't hesitate to refer to a professional if you need assistance with design. The easiest way to create an eBook is with the software called Scrivener. If you are creating a fixed eBook, you can create it in InDesign.

Understand professional formatting and book design.

You are able to use software provided by Amazon to create your book, but if you want to have your own personal design, we suggest you use Adobe InDesign. If your book is all text, then use what is easiest for you, but make sure your margins are sufficient, the text is readable, and the book looks as professional as possible. Self-published or not, more readers expect a book to look and feel a certain way. The time you put into making your title appear professional, the more likely it is that consumers will pick it up from the shelf.

Have an ISBN, barcode and a competitive price.

Buy your own ISBN at www.myidentifiers.com. You can make a barcode and embed the price within it. This helps if your book is going to be sold at brick-and-mortar stores. Create the barcode for free at this website www.creativindiecovers.com/free-online-isbn-barcode-generator/. Compare the price of your book to a similar book. If you are an equal in your field, set your price the same. If this is your first book and you just want to get your name out there, set your price a dollar or two below the average.

Get a website and use Amazon and Goodreads for promos.
Yes, you can sell your books only through other platforms, but having your own website allows you to keep more of the profit as well as collect emails from your faithful readers. Set up a website, start blogging and sell those books yourself.

Amazon allows you to set up an Author page which allows readers to see what you have done and it is free. So why not use it? Goodreads is another free service where you can interact with readers, do giveaways and get feedback on your book. (Remember not to take criticism too much to heart.)

With all our tips that we have shared with you, we have answered the question: But, couldn't I do that? The answer is yes. The only question left is: Do you want to?

CHAPTER TWELVE

But, Can I Really Do This?

The beautiful thing about self-publishing is that you can make as little or as much as you want of it. Do you just want to throw an eBook onto Amazon and call it a day? You got it. Want to self-publish an entire series and get the attention of Oprah? It'll be a battle, but why not? With the right armor and secret weapons, anything is possible. What matters most is your ability to persevere through the challenges, face adversities with strength and determination, and recognize that you may not be able to do it all. Lean on others, connect with the writing and publishing community, and trust yourself to know which direction you need to go.

Self-publishing is not for the faint of heart. It's not for the lazy, unmotivated, or weary. Self-publishing takes determination, enthusiasm, and courage. It takes a great idea, with great storytelling, and a great desire to put it out into the world. Consider the ways in which your work is integrated in the rest of your life. The more frequently that your book idea appears in your everyday life, the more successful you are bound to become. Why? Because it's no longer just a product or an idea, it's part of who you are and what you do. It's part of your identity.

People are going to challenge you, no matter what genre or subject matter you're writing about. They're going to question your motives and make you doubt yourself when it matters most. But those are not the voices that matter. Toni Morrison said, "If there's a book that you want to read, but it hasn't been written yet, then you must write it." There are tons of books out there about relationships, parenting, cyborgs, and talking frogs. But, if your version of those stories hasn't yet been told—if that book doesn't yet exist—write it. There are plenty of travel books out there, but Erin had her own unique perspective and experience to share. There are other books about television shows and movies, but Scott found an enthusiastic niche and an audience that craved his take on the productions. Just as there is always someone, somewhere, who would benefit from hearing your story or perspective, there is someone out there who will want to read your book.

You have something that others won't have. You have an idea and blueprint. We have given you advice we learned the hard way. You may disagree with some of the advice, and some of it you might take. Just write. Just create. Give the world a piece of you they didn't even know they were waiting for. Go write and be kind.

•••••

Erin: I didn't get into self-publishing and writing for the money. I would have been sorely disappointed if I had. I pursued the art form because I had a story that I felt could help change someone's perspective or simply brighten their life. At the end of the day, it wasn't the paycheck from book sales that brought me joy, it was the spontaneous Facebook messages or emails from readers telling me that I awoken something in them. It was the joy I could see in my audience's eyes as I shared with them the stories of Zeman and Tamara. It was the conversations that started as a result of my inviting someone into my journey. We could argue all day about the payoff of writing and publishing, but you will ultimately need to decide what's driving you to publish and why. Answering that question will not only indicate whether you're ready to take on the challenge, but may also help you step back and identify the subject matter that is most critical to who you are and what you do.

•••••

Scott: I became a writer because of the opportunities that arose and my desire to entertain strangers. That is who I am as a person. I wanted to contribute to the world of art. I wanted to inspire as I have been inspired.

I never dreamed of being the president of a publishing company or a managing editor of a magazine. All I ever dreamed of was creating art, and I have been able to do that. I can't wait for you to create yours.

📖 Honor Your Art

- Find ways to incorporate your book into other areas of your life
- Sales don't always equate to success
- Hitting "publish" is an accomplishment worth celebrating
- Attend book signings and author events, even if you're a small fish
- The world of publishing is continuously changing; be willing to change with it
- Brag about your book. You deserve it!

Your Golden Suitcase

There is a scene in Quentin Tarantino's 1994 masterpiece, *Pulp Fiction*, in which John Travolta and Samuel L. Jackson are driving along the highway arguing with Marvin, who is sitting in the backseat. John mistakenly shoots the poor sap in the face, blowing his head off and, therefore, blowing blood and guts all over the car. They don't want a cop to see this. They don't know what to do, so they pull off the highway and go to a friend's house and place a call to their boss. The boss sends Mr. Wolf, played by Harvey Keitel, looking so dapper in a tuxedo, at 9 in the a.m.

Mr. Wolf arrives, takes control of the situation, and all ends well—I mean, I guess not for Marvin, who's dead or John Travolta's character, who died before that or after depending on how hip you are—anyway, what does this have to do with you and me?

Well, you are John Travolta and Samuel L. Jackson (pretty good compliment, I say) and Erin and Scott are Mr. (& Ms.) Wolf. You see, in the end, all Mr. Wolf does is tell them to clean the car up. He doesn't really do anything. He just points the way, but it is John and Sam who are crawling in the backset picking bits of brain off the upholstery. They don't realize it because Mr. Wolf pointed them in the right direction just when they needed it the most. They aren't happy they have the dirty work, but let's be fair, they are the ones who got themselves into this mess.

There is no easy way to get out of a mess. And, make no mistake about it, publishing is a messy business—maybe not as messy as being hitmen, but it feels just as deadly. We look dashing and all tuxedo-ey in the a.m., and you feel like you are a bloody mess. We get it. We are here to point you in the direction. It is the best we can do. We hope you heard. We hope we helped. We want you to succeed, but in the end, it was always going to be you doing the dirty work. We probably will not know if you succeed, but we hope the path we cut for you is walkable, but it won't be without treachery, and it won't be easy. It was never our plan to slide into the back seat where the mess was. That was always on you. But we hope you push through the yucky parts and publish your fiction, whether it is categorized as pulp or not. Good luck with the mess, and drive safely.

MR. & MS. WOLF

Appendix A:
What Do Other Authors
Have To Say?

We asked a cross section of different authors at different levels of success and from different genres to answer 5 questions for us. The 5 questions were:

1. What is your name and what books have you written?

2. Did you self publish or go with a traditional publisher?

3. Why did you decide to go with them?

4. What was the best and worst part of your experience with that platform?

5. Would you recommend this way of publishing? What advice would you give to someone publishing their first book?

Over the following pages, we have listed their responses. We thank each author for taking the time to share their experiences with us. There is a lot of great advice here.

Brad Dukes

1. *Reflections: An Oral History of Twin Peaks*; *China Beach: A Book About a TV Show about a War.*

2. Self-published through Amazon.

3. Amazon made it easy. Writing is a passion—not a significant source of income for me. I bought my own ISBNs, used my own graphic designer, hired an editor, and tried to make it the most professional presentation possible. What I didn't get right on my first book, I was mostly able to improve on my second.

4. The best part is, it's just easy. I turned in two PDFs, and they do the rest—manufacturing, shipping. I literally sit back and get paid the royalties.

5. Honestly, I would because I have no understanding or comprehension regarding getting something published through a traditional house. It's a waste of my time. I'd rather be writing and exploring my creativity than venture into the black hole, void of soul, known as the world of publishing books. Write because you are truly passionate about your subject, not because you just want to write a book. The reader will know in an instant if you're a fraud.

Courtenay Stallings

1. *Laura's Ghost: Women Speak About Twin Peaks.*

2. I published with a small, independent publisher: Fayetteville Mafia Press.

3. I knew this particular publisher would support the work through the entire process from editing to promotion. It's difficult to get a contract with a big-name publisher when you're not a well-known writer with connections.

4. The best part of going with a publisher is they take care of the business and logistical aspect of publishing, which leaves me to concentrate on the creative side. The downside with going with a publisher is they do take a cut of the proceeds, which is understandable because of the nature of the work they are doing on behalf of your book.

5. For new or beginning authors, I would recommend they self-publish their works first in order to establish their name and credibility. For me, I had a good experience with Fayetteville Mafia Press because they are a small, independent publisher who makes it their mission to support independent writers who are not necessarily well-established yet. My advice to anyone publishing their first book is to get advice from other writers who have published books about the process and what works and what doesn't. Set up a logistical document to track your process and progress. Get feedback on drafts from an editor or someone you trust to provide constructive criticism. Don't be afraid to write a book that isn't perfect. Just do it. The first draft will be terrible, and that's OK. Once you see your published book, you'll have the pride of knowing you created something, and that's the best feeling there is.

~~~~~~

Lisa Mercado Fernandez

1. *The Shoebox, The Eighth Summer, Holding on to Hope,* and *Pieces of Home.*

2. I self-published the first with Abbott Press and the last two with BookBaby.

3. I decided to self publish because the task of finding an agent is grueling and disheartening. After years of pitching my books to countless literary agents it does a job on your self esteem. After years of trying I decided to put it out there on my own and make it happen.

4. With Abbott Press I felt harassed by their marketing department. I received three to four calls a week pushing me to sell my book. I was overwhelmed with the calls and emails and decided to drop them. After that I wrote two more books, and I began to pitch and query once again only to feel discouraged over time. BookBaby was an alternative that I was pleased with because I was still self-publishing but did not have to deal with the harassment and constant badgering about what I was doing to get my book out there.

5. As much as I am so happy with how my books were made and love having them, I'm literally right back where I began. My books have not reached the masses, not even close. As much as I have used social media and reached out to as many as possible, I could never do what a literary agent would do for me and the connections it would create with publishing houses and proper distribution. On the other hand, BookBaby has qualified and wonderful people working who literally hold your hand through the process. They are thorough and quick and, if you need a break from finding representation and want instant gratification, they will make your vision into reality.

~~~~~~

J.B. Minton

1. *A Skeleton Key To Twin Peaks, PoetrySexLife* (short stories, poems & essays), *… And The Third Floor Magistrates Took The Rape* (novel).

2. Self-publishing. For *PoetrySexLife and Magistrates*, I used Amazon Kindle KDP for the digital versions. For *A Skeleton Key*, I gave away all digital versions for free in exchange for gathering names and email addresses for my newsletter. Then I did a print-on-demand run with BookBaby that has opened up world wide distribution for print on demand.

3. For BookBaby, it was an easy decision. Because I was giving the revenue from the book away to charity, I needed the upfront capital to get the book into a print-on-demand revenue stream to be minimal. BookBaby has a minimum investment of 25 printed copies, but the more copies you order as an author/publisher, the cheaper the book price will be for the long tail of buyers who are going to get it through Amazon, Target, Barnes & Noble and through the BookBaby site. BookBaby does everything from accepting orders, printing orders, shipping orders and then paying the author royalties. With this setup, I write and design the book, produce the file and sit back and worry about marketing and collecting money.

4. Finalizing the design files sucked. It would have been really helpful to have an expert who I could pass that to. Now, BookBaby offers this as a service but that obviously increases the cost to the author. I will likely utilize this service for my next novel, as well as their cover design service. They do agency-level work that is on par with the major publishing houses.

5. I think many authors ignore the grunt work of producing enough content to gather an audience and then sell to that audience. Social media is a terrible way to centralize one's marketing efforts if there is no funnel to collect names and email addresses and then cater to that audience as the core readership. Any effort to utilize only online advertising is likely doomed to fail. I want a relationship with my readers, and I cater to this audience as the core of my efforts.

Charlotte Stewart

1. *Little House in the Hollywood Hills: A Bad Girl's Guide to Becoming Miss Beadle, Mary X, and Me.*

2. I had a traditional publisher with Bear Manor Media.

3. I chose them because their specialty is Hollywood, media personalities, etc.

4. They are very friendly when you order online but slow to deliver. They only do print-on-demand books, so they don't print a book until it is ordered.

5. I have friends who prefer self-publishing, but I was so new to it that I let my writing partner, Andy Demsky, choose everything.

~~~~~~~~~~~~~~~~~~~~~~~~~~~~~~~~~~

Mason Ball

1. The novel: *The Thirty-Five Timely & Untimely Deaths of Cumberland County*, Short story collections: *The Invention of Mother and The Lights Will Go Out, a fairy tale called The Menagerie* (illustrated by Jon Attfield) Poetry/prose collections : *Voices In The Red Velvet Elsewhere, Further Voices In The Red Velvet Elsewhere* and *Postcards From Twin Peaks*.

2. All but the novel are self-published. *Thirty-Five Deaths* was published by Unbound, a United Kingdom-based publisher that works on a crowd-funding model.

3. Quite simply I heard they were accepting submissions so I pitched the book to them, and they decided to go with it. This was after literally years of being rejected by traditional publishers and literary agents.

4. The editing process was tough, not because I was unwilling to "kill my darlings" but because, for some reason, the manuscript kept coming back to me with all new errors not present in the previous incarnation, and I began to feel like Sisyphus. All that was eventually solved though when I changed editors, and, in the end, my main issue with the process would be that once completed, Unbound did no promotion for the book and so actually getting it into the hands of readers fell to me. While I think I'm a pretty good writer, I am a lousy salesman.

5. I think I would still probably recommend publishing with Unbound, but only if the writer in question was willing and able to do the frankly ludicrous amount of legwork needed to promote their book.

As far as self-publishing the other books of mine, again, my advice is self-promotion isn't easy (and harder for some of us than others). What has helped me a little in this regard is that, as a cabaret performer, I have the platform to promote the things I've written and therefore gain an, albeit minuscule, audience from that.

~~~~~~~~~~~~~~~~~~~~~~~~~~~~~~~~~~

David Bushman

1. *Twin Peaks FAQ, Buffy the Vampire Slayer FAQ, Conversations with Mark Frost, Murder at Teal's Pond: The Mystery That Inspired Twin Peaks.*

2. Traditional: Applause Theatre & Cinema Books (An imprint of Hal Leonard LLC); Fayetteville Mafia Press; Thomas and Mercer.

3. One, they were willing to pay for it and to pay to market, promote, and distribute it. In the case of FMP, because I co-own it.

4. The distributor never does as much as you want it to. You have one book; they have hundreds. The same is really true of the publisher. You always want them to do more. But it is great that they sell to bookstores, libraries, and museums for you. I love that Hal Leonard/Applause got us signings at BookExpo. It's great to have access to a legal department and fact-checkers (provided by the publisher, not the distributor).

5. I would never recommend self-publishing, but rather a publisher that can pay you upfront and can provide a whole range of services—editing, fact-checking, promotion, legal, marketing, etc. I wish they did more, but whatever they do is more than I can ever do on my own.

Lindsay Hallam

1. *Screening the Marquis de Sade: Pleasure, Pain and the Transgressive Body in Film* (2012) *and Twin Peaks: Fire Walk with Me* (2018).

2. Traditional: I went with McFarland for my first book, and Auteur Press publishes the Devil's Advocates series.

3. I work in academia, so there is an expectation that I will publish work (books, chapters, journal articles) as part of having a university position. Most academics therefore go with a university press. I have some problems with this model, as academic books are usually very expensive, journal articles are often hidden by a paywall, and so your work is not really read that widely as the price makes it inaccessible.

McFarland is still considered to be in the area of academic publishing (although much of their output is not traditionally academic), but their books are much more reasonably priced. I ended up going with them because I had sent out a couple of proposals to different publishers, and they were the first to respond saying they wanted to do it.

For the second book, I really liked the Devil's Advocates series and thought it would be fun to write one. John Atkinson from Auteur often comes to conferences and sells books, so I spoke to him at one, and it went from there.

4. Most university presses are quite rigorous in reviewing your work and giving feedback, while McFarland basically published what I sent them. It was my first book, adapted from my Ph.D., and I had no idea what I was doing. Looking back, I think I would have really benefited from having some more guidance and peer-review. It's tough being critiqued, but it will always make your work better. Now I can see some flaws in the book, which I really wish someone had told me about back then!

With Auteur, the process was excellent. John Atkinson is the series editor and is always very responsive and understanding. It really helps to have a clear point of contact whom you can establish a relationship with and feel comfortable reaching out to whenever you have questions. It was also reassuring to have someone who checks in with you to see how it's all going.

5. This way of publishing is only really worth it if you are in academia. In order to maintain my position I am required to develop a good research profile. You cannot make a living from this alone; it's usually supplemented by your academic position. This goes back to my (many) problems with academic publishing—the books are so expensive, but as the author you get basically nothing! This is not the type of publishing where you get any type of advance. You may get some royalties but not much.

I also do some freelance writing work that is more like film journalism which I really enjoy. I get paid (again, not much), but I do it more for the love of it.

If you are a writer, you just have to write. If you're lucky you make a living from it, but that is increasingly rare. I would always try sending book proposals out to established publishers first before self-publishing, if only to get some feedback. From my experience you need critique, so send what you've done to mentors, friends, teachers, and colleagues who will be honest with you.

If no one bites but you believe in your work and think it's important to get it out there so you can move on to your next project, then do it through self-publishing. My most important recommendation, especially in this instance, would be to really increase your presence on social media and also create a blog or website. The main thing at the moment with so much stuff out there is to think about how to stand out and how people can find you. And get it reviewed wherever you can. Take this advice from someone whose first book came out and then disappeared into a void!

David Lee Morgan, Jr.

1. I have written eight books including *The Massillon Tigers: 15 for 15, LeBron James: The Rise of a Star*, and *More Than a Coach: What It Means to Play for Mentor, Coach, and Friend Jim Tressel.*

2. I did not self-publish any of my books. With my most recent book, *The Massillon Tigers: 15 for 15*, I went with Fayetteville Mafia Press.

3. I decided to go with Fayetteville Mafia Press because co-founders David Bushman and Scott Ryan were extremely enthusiastic in helping edit and design my manuscript. They understood how important the project was to me, and they did everything to make sure we produced an entertaining book.

4. As the author, I had a vision of how I wanted the book to be produced, from start to finish, and FMP had its own ideas that enhanced the project and added the right touches to make a quality finished project.

5. I would go with a traditional publisher. If possible, look for a publisher that is just as passionate about your project as you, and a company you can trust. It's that "gut feeling," you know, when you meet someone for the first time, and you can tell right away if you click or not. Go with your gut.

Marybeth Whalen

1. I've written nine novels, the first five were love stories set in Sunset Beach, North Carolina and the more recent four are what I call psychological fiction (read: people keeping secrets and not telling the truth). My most recent title is *This Secret Thing*, published in October 2020.

2. I went with a traditional publisher: Lake Union is the contemporary fiction division of Amazon Publishing.

3. Going with Lake Union meant I had the power of Amazon marketing behind my books. Also, they are very good to their authors.

4. The best part is having the Amazon algorithm working on my behalf. It's so fun to see your book release and climb the charts. I am not foolish enough to think that, as a beginning novelist in a crowded market, I could've ranked as high as I've gotten any other way.

The worst part is some snubbing that goes on within the industry—that somehow being published by Amazon is "less than" being published by the more recognized houses. So there are things you miss out on. But I knew that going in and made an informed decision.

5. I would recommend Lake Union—it affords opportunities that are otherwise hard to obtain within the competitive publishing industry. My best advice to anyone starting out would be to write that book you can't stop thinking about and give the process your all. Don't focus on the outcome until you've got a great book to show. When you start out, you might have some ideas about the direction you want to go, but the process of writing a book will teach you a lot—and you just never know where you'll end up.

Andreas Halskov

1. *Beyond Television: TV Production in the Multiplatform Era, TV Peaks: Twin Peaks and Modern Television Drama* and several anthologies.

2. The first two listed books are through University Press of Southern Denmark. The anthologies were self-published.

3. We chose to self-publish because there are not that many Danish publications about film and television.

4. The best thing about self-publishing is that you get to make and design your book on your own. That is both the most positive and negative thing connected to self-publishing. When working with a traditional publisher, you do not (typically) have to think about graphic design, editorial work, peer review, proofreading and distribution. Especially in terms of distribution, there is a problem with self-publishing, at least in Denmark, where the small distributors, which allow self-publishing, are unable to push your books and distribute them overseas. And the reviewers rarely even notice the books from small publishers.

5. Micro-publishers are becoming a thing these days, and the old-fashioned newspapers and popular media are slowly coming to understand that they need to take small publishers or untraditional media seriously. When you choose to self-publish, you short-circuit the traditional system, but your book still has to be noticed in the increasingly saturated marketplace, and that, sadly, depends on the interest from traditional media. If you choose to self-publish, it may be a good idea to ally yourself with competent people who can give you external advice and help you with all of the different aspects that you might not, yourself, be a master of: from editorial reviews and proofing to graphic design and promotion.

Ann Lewis Hamilton

1. *Expecting.*

2. I went with a traditional publisher: Sourcebooks.

3. I went with them because they wanted to buy my book!

4. The best? Being published. Wow, it was the dream of dreams. The editor was wonderful. I felt like F. Scott Fitzgerald and Maxwell Perkins. Well, sort of.

5. I would happily recommend this way of publishing. The advice I would give to someone publishing their first book: Spend the money; hire a publicist. You have to put your book out there. You have to be a cheerleader. Social media is your friend. This isn't the time to be shy. A flashing neon sign on your head saying, "Read my book!" is definitely the way to go.

Matthew Caracciolo

1. *The Waygook Book: A Foreigner's Guide to South Korea* and *Moon Ohio.*

2. Both my books are through traditional publishers: Monday Creek Publishing and Avalon Travel.

3. Because they accepted my book! As a debut writer, I didn't feel like I had the option to be choosey. For *Moon Ohio*, I applied for the opportunity to write a guidebook about my home state, and they hired me.

4. Monday Creek Publishing is a very small, local publisher. There aren't a ton of resources, and you have to do a lot of the work yourself, especially marketing. The flip side of the coin, though, is a very personal approach and devoted attention to your work from the publisher.

5. I know it's tempting to be impatient, but I would recommend giving an honest attempt at finding a real publisher before pursuing self-publication. I feel like having a real publisher's name on my book lends me a credibility that would be very difficult (though not impossible) to generate if my work were self-published. I'm also happy that I don't have to worry too much about most of the back-end stuff: legal language, contacting printers, and correct formatting.

About the Author: Scott Ryan

Written by Erin O'Neil

Scott Ryan is the author of *The Last Days of David Letterman, Moonlighting: An Oral History*, co-owner of Fayetteville Mafia Press, the Managing Editor of *The Blue Rose* magazine, an interviewer extraordinaire, and a number one fan of the Massillon Tigers. He is driven to create and produce, not because of fame or fortune (the latter of which is a moot point anyway), but because it keeps his heart pumping. A storyteller and entertainer by nature, Scott produces sparks of joy and inspires sincere kindness everywhere he goes. His affinity for turning a stranger's mundane afternoon into an unforgettable day is the truest form of art. He has an uncanny ability to turn an errand to the post office into a highlight of everyone's week, and a quick trip to Panera into a life-long friendship.

Despite the plague of what those who know him closest refer to as, "Scott Luck," Scott has managed to surround himself with good people, great music, and delicious pizza. His talents extend far beyond writing, publishing, and interviewing celebrities. He can also sometimes be found playing the piano, producing videos, and singing along with Barbra Streisand. Some of Scott's best decisions were marrying his wonderful life-partner, Jen, escaping the trenches of corporate cubicle work, and investing in a serious collection of vinyl records. He spends his downtime by the pool in the Sunshine State and kissing the ground on which Sheryl Lee walks. Oh, and of course, getting coffee and wearing robes with his best friend, Erin.

About the Author: Erin O'Neil

Written by Scott Ryan

Erin O'Neil is the author of *Gui Ren: Extraordinary Stories of Ordinary People*, the owner of Fishtail Publishing, a former board member of the National Storytelling Network, creator of Columbus Speaks, was picked as one of ILA's 30 under 30, and is addicted to ice cream. She is smart, beautiful, kind, and would cut a special agent for coffee in the morning, noon or night. She is madly in love with Josh Lovelien and her two cats. Although if you go to her house, it might seem like she has six cats. She knows software, has an eye for photography, can design anything, she will "cricut up" a piece of art in a moment, and writes so effortlessly, it could make a writing partner jealous. She has traveled the world, entertained countless audiences with her storytelling ability. She has hosted story slams and helped aspiring authors and storytellers find their inner plot.

She is getting married in 2021. She brings happiness and honesty to the world that is appreciated by everyone who knows her. Her path is just starting and where she ends up will be amazing. She loves her family just like they do in those old TV dramas and is a wonderful daughter to her parents. I know she can make your next project be even better than you ever imagined. Do yourself a favor and hire her. She can do anything she sets her mind to—anything but be your best friend because that position is already taken by me.

Special Thanks

Scott's Special Thanks: *Erin* is covered in her About the Author, but I'll thank her again for doing this project with me. *Courtenay Stallings* always is up for another one of my crazy projects. She has never told me no. I have to remember to ask her for a million dollars next time instead of launching another bad idea. *David Bushman* is a great partner in FMP, and I am glad we are braving this world of publishing together. I thank *Josh Lovelien* for allowing me to borrow his bride-to-be for hours of writing and eating. Thanks to *all the authors* whose books I mentioned and the ones who answered our questionnaire. Buy some of their books. Thanks to my wife, *Jen Ryan*, for always understanding that I am bound to go to Panera for coffee and come back with a new family member. I couldn't do any of this without her.

Follow Scott on Twitter: @scottluckstory @bluerosemag1
Email: Superted455@gmail.com (with kind comments only)
ScottRyanProductions.com

Erin's Special Thanks: My admiration and appreciation for *Scott* is unwavering, as is evident in his About the Author. Thank you to *Courtenay Stallings* for being our editor extraordinare and ganging up on Scott with me when it really counts. To *my grandparents* for gifting me a kid's self-publishing kit at age seven (who could have guessed it would turn into a career?). Thanks to *my family* for the steadfast support and trusting me to take a leap into self-employment at 24 and not end up in your basement. To *Jen Ryan,* for keeping not just one, but two quirky writers in your inner circle. Also, thanks for the bread. Thank you to *the authors and clients of Fishtail Publishing* for your business and friendship. My work wouldn't be possible without you. And to *Josh Lovelien,* for letting me bring a stray author from Panera into our home. P.S. Can we keep him?

Follow Erin on Instagram: @_itsonmylist @fishtailpublishing
Email: Fishtailpublishing@gmail.com (with kind comments only)
fishtailpublishing.org | erinoneil.org

One final thought: While we have you for a moment, we want to tell you about our religion. It is called kindness. All you have to do is be kind to everyone you meet. Double down on kindness to those who are different than you, those who don't like you, and those who have wronged you. It won't be easy, but you find that when you meet someone who has kindness in their heart, you will have the most wonderful relationship with them and the rest of the people will all fade away. Go be kind.

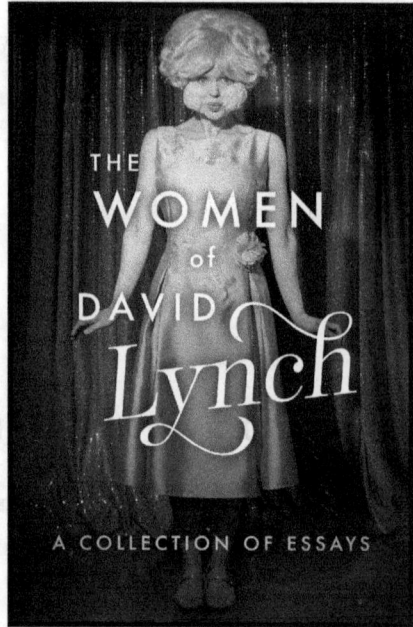

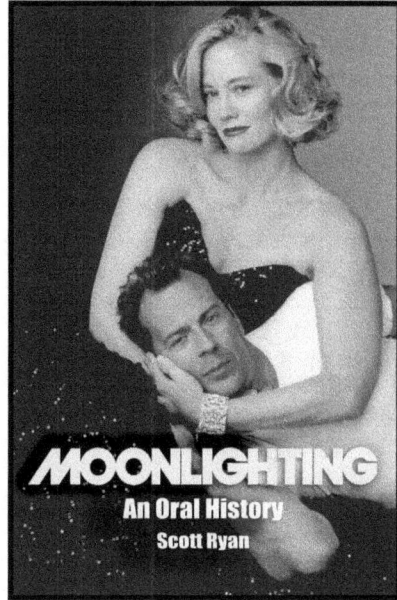

Moonlighting: An Oral History by Scott Ryan. Cybill Shepherd and Bruce Willis starred in one of the hottest shows in the eighties. Now the cast, writers and crew talk about how the series was made and what caused the show to end.

ISBN: 9781949024265

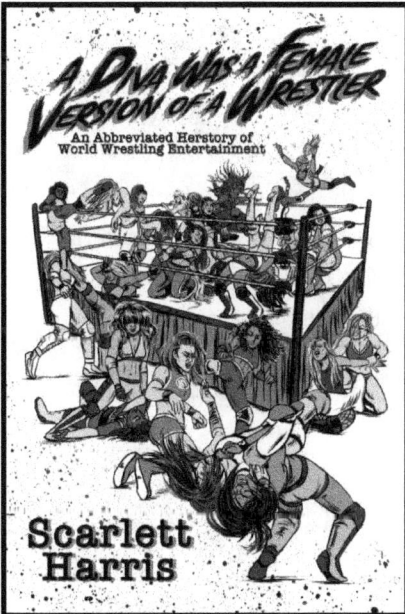

A Diva Was a Female Version of a Wrestler

Scarlett Harris takes a deep dive into the world of female wrestling and some of the greatest characters in all of sports.

ISBN: 9781949024180

Fire Walk With Me: Your Laura Disappeared
by Scott Ryan

A look at the 30th anniversary of David Lynch's *Twin Peaks* movie. Coming Summer 2022.

ISBN: 9781949024241

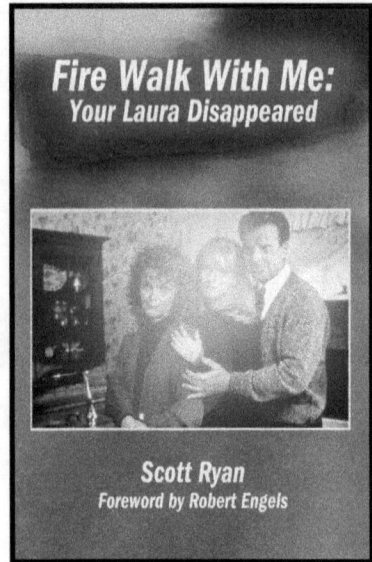

Fire Walk With Me:
Your Laura Disappeared

Scott Ryan
Foreword by Robert Engels

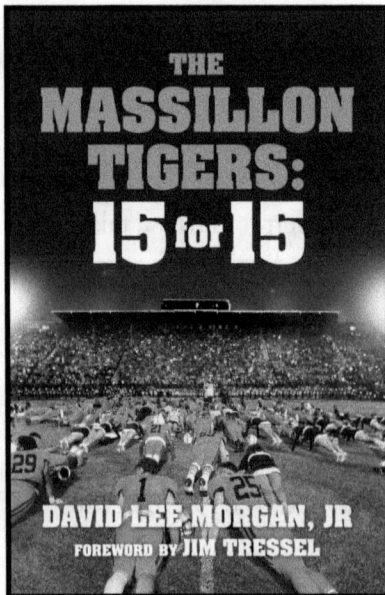

THE
MASSILLON
TIGERS:
15 for 15

DAVID LEE MORGAN, JR
FOREWORD BY JIM TRESSEL

The Massillon Tigers: 15 for 15 by David Lee Morgan, Jr., with a foreword by Jim Tressel. Follow along with the Ohio high school football powerhouse team the Massillon Tigers as they hunt for a state championship.

ISBN: 9781949024166

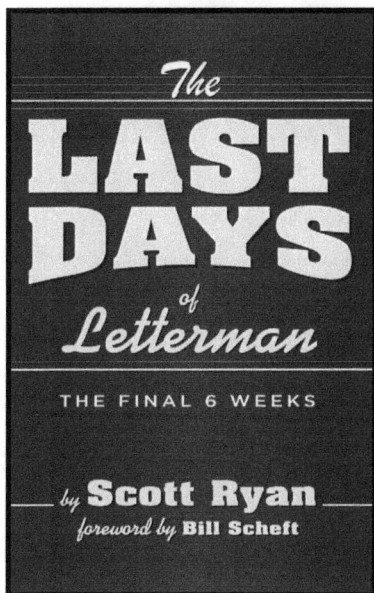

The Last Days of Letterman
by Scott Ryan

An inside look at the final six weeks of *Late Show with David Letterman,* all told through the words of the staff who wrote, directed, and produced those iconic last twenty-eight episodes in 2015.

ISBN: 9781949024005

Conversations with Mark Frost by David Bushman

Mark Frost cocreated *Twin Peaks,* wrote for *Hill Street Blues,* and has written over ten books. Learn about his life, his craft, and his career in this new book by David Bushman.

ISBN: 9781949024104

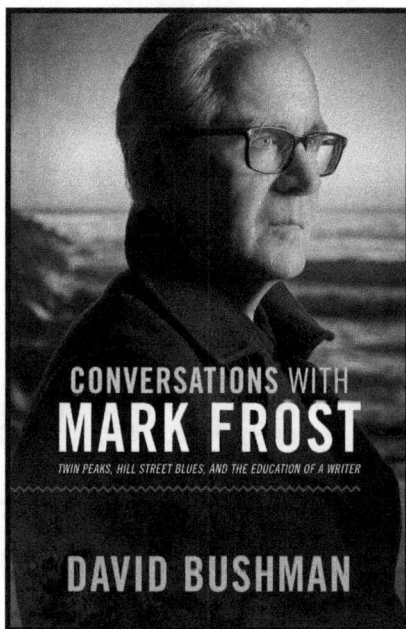

www.ingramcontent.com/pod-product-compliance
Lightning Source LLC
Chambersburg PA
CBHW060502280326
41933CB00014B/2825